M000236351

Growing Up
Barefoot
in Hawai'i

Growing Up Barefoot in Hawai'i

by
Peggy Hickok Hodge

Copyright © 1997
by Mutual Publishing

No part of this book may be reproduced in any form or by any
electronic or mechanical means, including information storage and
retrieval devices or systems, without prior written permission from the
publisher, except that brief passages may be quoted for reviews.

All rights reserved
Library of Congress Catalog Card
Number: 96-78337

First Printing May 1997
97 98 99 00 01 02

Softcover
ISBN 1-56647-138-9

Mutual Publishing
1127 11th Avenue, Mezz. B
Honolulu, Hawaii 96816
Telephone (808) 732-1709
Fax (808) 734-4094
e-mail: mutual@lava.net

Designed by Kennedy & Preiss Graphic Design
Printed in Australia

The title of this nostalgia could also have read
"Growing Up Barefoot in Hawai'i...
and so did my kids and grandkids."

A Kaleidoscope of Memories
Table of Contents

I Remember

I grew up in Kaimuki, which was considered its own town back then, and not a suburb of our fair city.

Everything I remember about Honolulu and the island of O'ahu from the old days, I could never contain in just one book. But what I remember best is here.

I remember how hot Kaimuki's first paved roads were. The black macadam looked and felt like a parched Kona lava field. The main street parallel to Wai'alae Avenue was named for President Harding, who had just died.

And I remember:

When Wilhelmina Rise was bare, except for a footpath up the middle of overgrown sisal trees and carnation plants.

When there were new sidewalks along the pavement, and we roller-skated down sixteen blocks of smooth cement to Ali'iolani School. And my sister and I won all the first prizes for roller-skating, girls under 12 on the streets at Bingham Tract near the University of Hawai'i (with four new buildings as its campus), and we trekked up there to test the latest concrete surfaces.

When everything about Honolulu seemed so wide open, compared to now. You could ride down Kalakaua Avenue in an old open-sided electric street car and see the entire beach

My dad paid $1,500 for this completely furnished Kaimuki home where I grew up.

at Waikiki with all of Diamond Head before you, an expansive scene fringed with coco palms planted for royalty in the largest grove on Oʻahu.

When the sun rose and shone on Waikiki bay's churning breakers. Canoe paddlers and surfers rode in majestically, passing by schools of green sea turtles.

When the Moana was the only hotel on the beach. Its pier and gazebo lured lovers out for a bit of romantic "spooning." The beach was narrower then, and the sand was very white. There were no rope or chain barriers to reserve sunning space for tourists, and no one hunted coins and jewelry with noisy mechanized metal detectors to disturb the serenity of diners at waterfront tables.

When membership at the modest Outrigger Canoe Club cost only $10 a year for the family and included six free guests a month. Duke Kahanamoku and the beach boys shared homemade stew with us at the club and taught me to surf and play the ʻukulele.

When all of Oʻahu was a mass of green, speckled with brilliant shower trees, hibiscus and plumeria. All businessmen in town wore coats and ties, and ladies donned hats and gloves when they traveled to Honolulu.

When the road ended at Kuliʻouʻou and you had to walk barefoot over Koko Head with all your gear for an evening supper picnic at Hanauma Bay, and we enjoyed freshly caught mullet, "two for a quatta," pulled from the circular throw nets of Hawaiian fishermen.

When you could find whole shells on the sand of the remote beaches on the North Shore and leeward sides of Oʻahu.

When plumerias were called "graveyard flowers" because they grew in cemeteries and were considered too common and cheap for leis, but today they are highly prized.

When "high tea" at the Damon Estate's Moanalua Gardens was the big event every Sunday afternoon, highlighted by a fashion show, with the ladies parading in their long skirts and blouses, and sporting upswept coiffures and plumed chapeaux under dainty parasols.

When all the unfenced Waikiki Zoo had was our beloved elephant Daisy, a chimpanzee named Jenny, two lions, and a few molting camels and you held your nose riding the trolley over the McCully bridge to Waikiki because of the awful stench from smelly duck ponds below.

When a nickel, one-third of a week's allowance, could buy a loaf of bread, or a bag of crackseed, a big molasses candy bar, a Saturday movie matinee, a newspaper, a bottle of milk, or an ice cream cone.

When we slept overnight on the ground as we waited for the flyers to come through Kolekole pass in the Dole Derby. Only two out of eight made it across the Pacific in 1927.

When the old streetcar clanged down Wai'alae Avenue to town and you could see all the way to the Wai'anae range with Mt. Ka'ala looming in the distance, with nothing in between but tropical palms, flowering trees, and hedges of oleander or red, pink, and white hibiscus.

When Island transportation was by ship and everyone rushed to Pier 2 for nostalgic, tearful alohas. The Royal Hawaiian Band and falsetto voices pierced the air with haunting melodies. Colorful streamers waved from ship to shore. On a departing liner the passengers would throw leis overboard to ensure a return to the Islands.

When Hawai'i was what Somerset Maugham portrayed: visions of sloe-eyed Polynesian maidens peering through slats of bamboo blinds in cozy cottages.

Growing Up in Kaimuki

I was a little girl, sitting on the dusty ground at the edge of our bouldered lane in Kaimuki, digging my bare toes in the fine, warm, red lava dirt, and watching steam shovels gouge out parched chunks of earth. Our town was about to move into the modern world with paved roads, complete with cement curbs and sidewalks. When the steamrollers came through, we kids followed alongside and picked up tar and chewed it by the mouthful.

My dad made me my own steam shovel (that really worked) out of an orange crate, tin cans, and wires. I could sit in it and pull small rope gears that enabled me to dig up soil and carry it away. The only thing missing was the hiss of the steaming motor, and the nearby steamroller.

But all at once we had smooth speedways for riding scooters and roller-skating with few cars around. So many avenues: the steep, new Harding Avenue, parallel to historic Wai'alae Avenue, where the streetcar ended at the bottom of Koko Head Avenue.

From our hilltop home in Kaimuki we could watch the moon rise over Maunalua Bay at the foot of Koko Head. There were no houses in between, just a view of the tops of tropical trees, bathed like leafy orbs in the moonlight.

We learned astronomy from a Bishop Museum scientist who talked to us on what we called Star Hill, where the large Punahou School telescope was set up among the lava boulders. Children, parents, and dogs strolled in the evening to the weekly show, and everyone would ooh and aah over the magnified stars and planets.

All we needed for games in those days were a few sharp sticks, some rocks and some marbles. We'd draw fish outlines in the dirt for marble shoots, line up the colorful agates and carefully balance thumb against forefinger to shoot. First one to aim and "kill" the marbles in the fish won, and could pick up all the marbles as the prize.

"Steal eggs" was a more complex game. You tried to get your foot inside a large enemy circle a few yards from yours without getting tagged, steal a rock and take it back to your circle. The winner was the one with the most rocks.

We also played "Hopscotch" in the dirt on squares drawn with sticks where pebbles were thrown into a square ahead of us. We'd hop forward on one leg until we stopped in an adjacent square to pick up the pebbles—while still standing on one foot!

Another pastime was gluing small milk tins to the bottom of our feet with the sap from a green klu pod, and pretending to walk around on stilts.

We played clown with sticky hibiscus stamens pasted on our noses and torn-off petals stuck to our cheeks.

We often squirted one another with the gooey sap of green tulip tree pods after we bit off the ends. Or we would take a large woodrose seed, which had a velvety black line across the top, rub it hard on rough cement (the friction made it sizzling hot), and sting an opponent with it. Ouch!

Another pastime was following around the boys when they were shooting their cap pistols. We girls weren't allowed to own cap guns. They were loaded with rolls of powder-dotted red paper and made a firecracker bang when the hammer hit a dot. We'd scavenge the unspent shots and explode them on rocks by pounding stones on them.

We also gathered up the red unlaunched firecrackers left on the road. We'd bend them in half to expose the gunpowder, and light them with matches we had secretly stolen from the kitchen. The powder made a fizzing noise and spewed out golden sparkles.

Sometimes we played Indians in khaki-colored costumes of fringed skirts and vests, and large feather headbands. Mostly we girls just danced around imitating pictures in *National Geographic* magazine.

The earth was always warm and sometimes even too hot for unshod tender feet, so I'd skip from one mound of morning glory vines to another, collecting monarch butterfly caterpillars. I'd put the caterpillars in a jar and later watch them metamorphose, and let them fly away when their beautiful orange and black wings were dry.

Growing up barefoot was a callused, blistered affair. But feet became almost as useful as hands. With a stick held between my sturdy toes I could draw the fish for our marbles game, or hopscotch squares, or a smiling face to adorn the soft ocher volcanic soil of Kaimuki.

My prehensile toes allowed me to pick up most anything: zori sandals (two at a time), marbles, small O'Leary rubber balls, combs, pencils, and even sea bird feathers on the sand. Also crabs, coral. And shells, even if they had to be dug out, like the auger shells in the shorebreak at Pupukea, or the slippery cowries in the lettuce seaweed along the reef at Ma'ili Beach on leeward O'ahu.

We often played a singing game with our feet as we reclined in our big lanai hammock. Each girl lay on her back facing the other and matched soles of feet, then while singing we "bicycled" back and forth together, like pumping a player piano.

Our chores at home—besides cleaning the house, feeding the chickens, and watering the plants—included weeding for pay, 10 cents a bucket. This meant pulling out the roots, which we did with agile toes pinched together. A bonus was eating the succulent pigweed afterwards.

When we realized how much faster the job could be with a rabbit, we'd leash one and let him munch on the weeds, but pull him back when he got ready to gobble any nearby flowers.

One indelible memory is running barefoot down our lava dirt road to visit my Hawaiian friends. Their garden had an enormous mulberry tree whose berries we picked and bit to get juice for make-believe lipstick that turned our lips a ghoulish mauve-blue. For this delightful escapade, I was duly spanked by my mom and leashed to an avocado tree!

There were ten kids in that Hawaiian family and a happy, generous mom who always wanted to feed me.

I learned to eat everything and was welcomed as their *keiki* (child) and joined in the family circle on the *lauhala* mat, plunging my tiny fingers in the poi bowl and trying a bit of raw fish, dried shrimp, eel, octopus, and *limu* (seaweed).

Almost every morning, as soon as my sterile breakfast of prunes, oatmeal mush, and boiled egg was over, I would hightail it to their house to eat an *'ono* (delicious) Island-style offering of butter-fried eggs, Portuguese sausage, and rice.

Me, the little one on the right, growing up barefoot with Hawaiian friends at Hale'iwa, 1918.

Their father was the first professor of the Hawaiian language at the new University of Hawai'i, and my dad was the first vice-principal and science teacher at McKinley High School, the only public high school on O'ahu then, and I was the first baby born to McKinley faculty! Anyway, that was how our parents knew each other.

The *kupuna* (grandma) of the family had long, flowing gray hair and spoke only Hawaiian. With dramatic gestures, she would interpret signs in the sky for us. I learned many island legends from her and later, in my graduate studies in Pacific mythology, I authored a booklet of my favorite Hawaiian stories.

The *kupuna* had predicted a tragic omen, and it happened soon afterwards—Queen Lili'uokalani's death. One morning, dressed in hat and shiny Mary Jane shoes, I rushed with my mother in her long skirts and parasol to join the crowds watching the royal funeral.

The Queen's body lay in state at Kawaiaha'o Church. Hawaiian ladies in rustling black taffeta gowns and orange leis of the native *o'o* bird were wailing and chanting in the traditional Hawaiian manner. My dad marched in the funeral cortege as a government official. I waved my tiny Hawaiian flag when the procession rolled by. Stevedores pulled the casket all the way up Nu'uanu Avenue for burial in the Royal Mausoleum.

As I held my mother's gloved hand, she squeezed my fingers and solemnly whispered, "Never forget this moment. She is the last Queen of your land."

Back in Kaimuki we kids returned to our school and play, but I never would forget the solemnity and majesty of the Queen's funeral.

Kaimuki was like Kona in those days—hot and dry, with *kiawe* trees everywhere. We used to gather the long, slender, yellow *kiawe* beans in burlap sacks and sell them for 10 cents, a big addition to our 15-cent-a-week allowance. The pods smelled like sweet hay and were used as cattle fodder.

Folks who lived in mildewy valleys like Nu'uanu and Manoa had second "summer homes" in Kaimuki to dry out in the rainy winter days.

Bare feet carried us kids up the mountain behind Kaimuki. It was named Wilhelmina Rise after the Kaiser's queen. But, when World War I erupted and we were fighting the Germans, it was called Sierra Heights. The new development being built on the slope was called Maunalani. When World War I came, my mother made me a "Red cross uniform" and I helped her roll bandages.

We kids used to sing a ditty about our German enemy to the tune of "Jack and Jill" (a *puka* is a hole):

> Kaiser Bill went up the hill
> to fetch a pail of water;
> He fell down with a frown
> with *puka* pants thereafter.

The footpath straight up the middle of the mountain wove through overgrown sisal plants, originally planted there for a rope industry that failed. Fields of red and pink carnations flourished and smelled like the docks on Boat Day. Realtors were selling entire blocks for $500 on The Mountain, envisioning roads with utilities circling Maunalani Heights, which eventually materialized into expensive house lots. My dad thought about buying a lot, but my conservative mom chided him: "Ben, what do you want all that red dirt for?" So Dad never joined the *hui* (groups of businessmen), as he never thought it right to make money off the land.

We ran uphill like goats and finally came to the top, where the unmarked, unfenced Lanipo Ridge trail began. The foot-wide slippery trail was scary, dropping off hundreds of feet to the valleys below on either side. Today those valleys are studded with homes, row on row.

We climbed up and down on rough lava dikes, carefully holding on to *puka* (holes) in the outcroppings; we had to grab really hard with our fingers and toes! This was where we'd find "Hawaiian diamonds" (mica) and real Hawaiian olivines, not the fake plastic kind manufactured and sold today as olivine in local jewelry stores.

When we ran farther up the precipitous tops of the trail, we wedged our barefoot toes through *uluhe*

Me, in my World War I "Red Cross Uniform."

(brittle false staghorn fern) that engulfed the mountains like a fishnet drawn taut. Often we'd just fall back and lie in the cool, damp fern and watch tiny spiders weave delicate webs and catch unwary insects. Far beyond were open grassy meadows with dwarfed *'ohi'a* trees with red pompom blossoms, *tabu* (forbidden) for picking or it would rain, legend warned.

On the way back we'd stop and look at the magnificent far view of the sea, and right into the crater of Diamond Head (what Hawaiians and locals call Le'ahi). Le'ahi was unspoiled and detached from civilization, truly a historical monument, robed only in a fresh, green, grassy mantle after the heavy rains. The mountains and valleys stretched for miles, filled with plunging waterfalls and vibrant rainbows.

We bounced downhill on the single trail that later became the main thoroughfare for the tiered paved drives of fashionable and expensive Maunalani Heights. Far below to the east lay Honolulu Harbor, with its steamships and rigged sailing vessels, and straight out we had a view of the quagmired duck swamp encircling Waikiki. This was before the land barons built the Ala Wai Canal to drain out the stagnant mosquito-laden still waters at the end of Kapahulu Road.

Our bare feet became permanently sienna-soiled, making it impossible to get them clean beneath toenails, even though the constant soaking in salt water with daily swims at Kahala or Waikiki helped. How long I would sit in the tub and scrub my feet. Dad designed a sun heater for the top of our house, and it produced boiling hot water after noon for our late baths. I could float in that seven-foot bathtub with all the hot water I wanted. I used to think our long, white bathtub was a real live thing because it had clawed feet; sometimes at night when I'd hear strange sounds, I imagined the tub creature was sneaking out of the house because it got its bottom scoured too hard and often!

But eventually the iron-rich dirt of Kaimuki seeped into the porcelain of the tub and gave it a permanent reddish cast that defied even the strongest cleanser. I think the same thing happened to me. After so many years bounding around barefoot on the mud-squishy trails, I have been imbued with the indelible, fundamentally common beauty of our island's richest soils. And those barefoot days hold some of my fondest memories.

My Historic Birthplace

Princess Kekaulike had deeded her home to be used for the first Kapiʻolani Maternity Home "to propagate and perpetuate the race" as King Kalakaua had decreed when he came to power. He had appointed Queen Kapiʻolani to head the society to work on accomplishing this task. She dreamed of founding a maternity home to care for poor Hawaiian mothers and their babies. The hospital which opened in 1890 was dedicated to the mothers of Hawaiʻi and named after Kapiʻolani. It was a rambling cottage of five bedrooms beneath *kiawe* trees and coco palms in Honolulu during World War I at the Diamond Head corner of Keeaumoku and Beretania Streets.

There were openings for non-Hawaiians who could pay as patients and I was born there in 1914. The Hawaiian women were suspicious of *haole* (foreign) doctors and institutions and preferred having their babies birthed at home in the traditional manner. Only six babies were born in the new hospital when it opened in 1890.

Kamaaina women brought fresh produce and baked goods from their own homes and volunteers helped wash the diapers. Every week ten gallons of poi came by cart from the taro patches deep in Manoa Valley, now covered with homes.

During World War I patients were charged $1.50 for the doctor's taxi fare from Queen's Hospital in town to the new hospital in Makiki. A private room cost $6 a day, plus $10 for the delivery room and $2.50 for laundry. Folks without money contributed fish, taro, and vegetables.

Our Stores

The few stores we had were centered around the end of the trolley line at the top of Wai'alae Avenue. Each of these Chinese mom-and-pop stores had its specialty besides fresh fruits and vegetables.

There was the butcher shop where mother would send me for 75 cents' worth of cut sirloin steaks for the family of six!

I loved watching the gold-toothed butcher walk into his huge, cold-storage warehouse, unbolt the heavy wooden doors with metal locks and take out a hanging beef carcass. He wore a heavy, white cotton apron splattered with blood, and the floor was covered in sawdust, which helped to soak up the blood as it dripped from his large, wooden cutting table. He used his sharp cleaver like a tennis racket to hack off chunks of the fresh red Parker Ranch meat, and then he'd slice it with a large hacksaw and long carving knife.

He wrapped the fresh meat in thick butcher paper, with the price scribbled outside in large Chinese characters. Then he put a sheet of paper with a small duplicate of the Chinese words through the big pointed spindle on the counter before handing me the moist package.

Chinese peddler selling bananas from the back of his donkey. Bishop Museum

Sometimes Mother allowed me to buy a box of dried lychee nuts or some candied squash, coconut strips, or kumquats for dessert, but never boxes of rich chocolate creams. For sweets, Dad bought us chunks of hard milk chocolate, which he kept in a huge glass jar with a very tight lid. When he inspected the candy store during a shopping stop, we kids walked down the long line of tempting trays, often tasting the hand-dipped cherries and caramels as we went.

At the Chinese store the bookkeeper would sit on a high stool and tally up our purchases on an abacus that echoed softly with brown beads on metal bars. His nimble fingers could match any computer checkout today.

Nobody weighed fruit by the pound. Bananas were a dime a bunch, large papayas a dime each, and juicy, golden-ripe pineapple another ten cents. I carried everything home in my cart, bumping up and down in the dusty dirt road. If it rained, the grocer would open up his oil-slicked Oriental umbrella painted with birds and butterflies, under which I huddled as I headed toward home.

Vegetable Lady

More exciting than the grocery store for us kids was the beloved "Vegi'bul Lady" who came by in her high wagon pulled by a sometimes lazy horse, or perhaps it was a mule.

We knew she was coming down the hill when we heard the clippety-clop of horse hooves. She was a large Okinawan woman with a ruddy complexion and long black hair pulled into a bun, topped by a large-brimmed straw hat secured with a red bandanna scarf. Her hands were worn rough from riding without gloves, and she held a long bamboo stick to gently guide the horse's gait. Her apron of coarse cotton was worn and usually soiled from the dirt in the vegetable roots. Sometimes she let us feed her horse from a bag under its head. We loved to reach in for the feed that smelled like freshly mown grass and herbs.

Her cart overflowed with fresh vegetables just uprooted from the truck farms in Kahala, and with wonderful local fruits: the buttery green things we called "alligator pears," later known as avocados, and the homegrown mangoes, soursop, mountain apples, pineapples, limes, lemons, Kona oranges, thick cooking bananas, papayas, and slip-skin Isabella black grapes good for making preserves or jam.

She also had packages of crisp chocolate cookies, Nabiscos, Graham crackers, and large Pilot crackers that came in tins. Hidden around the edges of her cart were paper-wrapped molasses bars and peppermint chews, which she gave to us kids when Mother wasn't looking.

Barber Shop

There was one barber shop in the village. We always stopped to watch the big, bright red-and-white circular pole turning like a giant peppermint candy stick. We'd peer in the glass to watch the for-men-only shop (as all the girls and women wore long hair).

A shave and haircut was really only two bits. The Japanese lady barbers were dressed in kimonos, with their long sleeves tucked in their *obi*. They used hand clippers and long scissors for short, neat cuts, and large open razors for a shave, slapping the steel back and forth on heavy leather strops to make the blades as sharp as samurai swords.

We often waited for our dad in the barber shop. Even though we couldn't read the Japanese newspapers, pulp magazines, and cartoons with fierce horse-riding, sword-wielding Japanese war lords doing terrible things, we loved looking at the pictures.

Dad used to say it should have cost more to cut his balding head because it took so long to find the hairs!

Yardage Shop

Our Japanese neighbors, the Takao Ozawas, founded the shop that grew into the Kaimuki Dry Goods Store, run by his family. The original store was stocked with soft cotton voile, shiny poplin, Indian head, and one-of-a-kind buttons. For silk we had to go to Chinatown.

Later the college-educated daughters carried on in the large, new Kaimuki Dry Goods Store frequented by fashionable women throughout Oʻahu. The store has sponsored chic fashion shows in Waikiki hotels that showed gowns made with their fabrics and accessories.

Today Dee Dee Miyashiro, granddaughter, manages the store.

The Crackseed Store

Forbidden to us by our father, Territorial Food Commissoner and Analyst, was the crackseed store! But, in spite of being warned that the delicacies were sometimes unclean and full of rat droppings that even killed one boy, we sneaked in before the Saturday matinee and secretly bought our lumpy-full bags for a nickel each.

Huge glass jars on the floor and low shelves were filled with various succulent seeds from Hong Kong. The colors and shapes of every variety intrigued us endlessly. The jars were smudged with tiny fingerprints from the gooey hands of kids tasting the different flavors.

The delicacies were shoved into brown paper sacks and immediately began to seep through in an intriguing gelatinous manner, far surpassing in sensual delight the weighed-to-the-ounce, computer-price-tagged sealed plastic bags hanging on check-out counters of supermarkets today.

Sometimes we also bought a full bag of pine nuts. We

knew how to snap them open and to sort kernels from the loose shells in the dark at the picture show.

We usually visited the crackseed store on Saturdays before the afternoon movie matinee at the new Kaimuki Theater down the hill. As we purchased our delicacies, we could hardly wait to see the continuing series of Tarzan, who had been pursued by gorillas and left hanging on a cliff, or Tom Mix in his chase with Indians, or Buster Keaton teetering on the ledge of a high building that was falling apart!

My piano teacher played the organ for these silent movies, and he pulled out all the stops and wildly crescendoed the music to match the breathtaking climaxes on screen. After my weekly lessons he would let me sit beside him before the huge pipe organ in the empty theater, and I would play the manuals while he did the footwork with the pedals. Right then I decided I wanted to play for the movies, but reviewing them in later life was as far as I got. And by then we had talkies and no need of organists.

Consuming crackseed in our day took a certain degree of skill. We squeezed out the round cracked seeds like rare delicacies. The hard circles of yet undetached seeds we would swirl with our tongues with a primitive sucking sound. The art was to bite into the cracked seeds and, without using fingers, crunch into the heart to extract the tender almondy kernel and get the meaty parts off the exterior, swallow the edible parts and then almost simultaneously spit out the dry shells separately. If we were outside, gorging ourselves before the next streetcar came, we spat out the hard shells on the ground. But if indoors, we cupped our hands and transferred the shells to a napkin or handkerchief to empty later in the trash barrel.

The proverbial last lick was when the bag was presumably finished. Then the owner of the bag would tear the flavor-sogged paper with lingering shreds of crackseed into equal shares for her friends. We took the roughly torn pieces into our mouths and sucked until every bit of the seeds' tang was gone!

Crackseed has a unique flavor of licorice, ginger, and other spices blended in a characteristic sweet-sour sauce. During World War II when we couldn't get it from the Orient, we tried making it with raw prunes cracked and marinated in sugar, salt, fresh ginger, and anise condiment, but it never came out the same, except for the soft almond-like, tender inner seed.

My favorite was the mashed seed of an Oriental plum, preserved in a sweet-and-sour anise-flavored sauce that was the delight of all island kids. Even when you left for college, you sneaked packages or tins in your footlocker between books and woolen clothes.

Besides these seeds, there were the more bland, long strips of stringy mango seed dyed red, whole seedless cherry seed, seedless whole seed, dry sweet-sour seed, Japanese plums wrapped in leaves and soaked in an addictive brine solution, and the many kinds of glazed candied fruit and vegetables used as dessert at Chinese feasts, along with large, crumbly, almond wedding cookies and fortune cookies. *See moi (Li Hing Mui),* the saltiest of all the seeds, was one you could never put whole right into your mouth; it was so stingingly salty, with large grains of Oriental rock salt all over the outside. So you held the seed gingerly in your fingers and cautiously bit off tiny pieces that still made you wince. If you ever saw some kid, clutching a small brown paper bag, with tears running down his cheeks, you knew he was eating *see moi.*

It took another studied talent and strong teeth to eat a bag of the tiny island dried shrimp, which we also bought for a nickel. You shook out a few of the stiff, dried red shrimp into your eager mouth to soften them up with saliva, and let them marinate in your puffed-out cheeks before slowly chewing them side-to-side with a bovine cud mastication, extracting all the true shellfishy flavor before you finally swallowed.

Shave Ice

Next to the crackseed store was "shave ice," another island delicacy. Kids lined up in front of a stand where an Oriental vendor was actually shaving thin wafers of ice by hand from a huge block. He used a shaver that looked like one used for lumber. He filled a paper cone to the brim and poured over the sugary-sweet syrup of the buyer's choice. You took a long time to decide which one of the large glass bottles of syrup to choose: bright-pink strawberry—everyone's favorite, that made your tongue a circus red—or orange, lemon, and, later, root beer or Coke.

You stood on one foot, then another, as you made the biggest choice of your day. Sometimes you made two syrup selections and the colors might blend into a bizarre, sea-sickening green shade! And you would suck the juice down to the bottom of the cone with a great audible slurp!

It always took a long time to finish that magic cornucopia of sweetness, and the color you had chosen usually dripped on to the pinafore you wore, and the dye would not come off with Mother's bluing ball for bleach!

A Nickel Went Far

A nickel went such a very long way in those days... a loaf of bread, a whole bag of crackseed, or a bag of pine nuts from Japan, a molasses candy bar, the Saturday matinee at the Kaimuki Theater.

Five cents was one-third a week's allowance, and it could buy a newspaper, and was one of five to make a "quatta" (two bits) for a proverbial "shave and haircut."

No one had to weigh fruit and vegetables. Ripe yellow papayas (if none were ripe on your own trees) were two for a dime or five for a "quatta." If we did pick them from the trees in our yard, we kids sometimes used the hollow stems of the papaya leaves for blowing bubbles from a frothy soap mixture in a kitchen bowl or from a bathtub.

A hand of bananas seldom cost more than a nickel and never came with an Ecuador sticker and green-to-ripen-at-home. Most folks grew their own anyhow. We had bananas galore to eat in peanut butter and mayonnaise sandwiches, on cereal, in between meal snacks, and cooked with brown sugar, butter, and orange juice. We ate cooked bananas with fish and meat, or as a dessert over homemade ice cream.

A nickel would also buy puffed rice candy squares with peanuts, or the tooth-extracting gelatinous-based gooey kind covered with sesame seeds. Those were usually only five for a nickel, now 75 cents each! There were no labels on the goods because no one knew for sure what was in the concoctions, but my dad at the Board of Health had forbidden us to eat the stuff.

A nickel ice cream cone was piled high with two scoops, but usually you couldn't get anything but vanilla, chocolate, and strawberry.

Canned evaporated milk, used for babies' formula and in lieu of bottled fresh milk by many families, was only a nickel.

A big tin of red sockeye salmon was only three nickels.

Hamburger was only three nickels a pound and always freshly ground.

And the old electric trolley car was a nickel before we had to buy tokens for seven cents.

Sounds

I can't remember a time when a gecko, or speckled brown house lizard, didn't make a sound as I dozed off to sleep or awoke to a new day. The geckos clicked or chirped in the eaves of my room with a song like staccato castanets of smooth stream pebbles rhythmically beaten together. There was the fox gecko with his long narrow nose, who would lie flat, waiting on glass windows, floors, or ceilings for errant moths, flies, or ants to catch and eat.

We'd find lizard eggs precariously slid into narrow door-jambs, under the felt pads over the hammers (warmed by heaters) in the piano, or behind books on the shelves. The little white ovoids were like miniature eggs ready for an Easter hunt.

The cooing of the doves began at day-break, the large lace-necked dove with its strong, low "coo coo coo," followed by the smaller zebra dove in higher staccato notes, each answered by an attending mate.

Ready for a ride in the Model T Ford with me in the middle window at age five, 1919.

In the still of the night from our Kaimuki home down the lane of what is now Koko Head's freeway exit, I heard the lions roar at the zoo and shuddered beneath my bed clothes, remembering when Daisy the elephant broke her chains and got loose and everyone said she might tear open the lions' cage and they would eat us up!

I can still hear the sound of the ice man's heavy wet dungarees squeaking, rubbing one leg against the other, as he came up the back path carrying, with large sharp tongs, a heavy, dripping block of ice. The block never fit inside the old brown wooden icebox, so he had to get out his big ice pick and shear it off to fit, as we waited beside him to catch the crystalline pieces and suck them.

I remember the sound of the streetcar as it warmed up, and I memorized those special noises... "klonkety, klonk! klonkety klonkety, chukka chukka!"

And there was the sound of the old Model T being cranked outside by Dad as he let me, at age 4, adjust the steering wheel levers for the gas; and the sound of butter being churned during World War I; or the ice cream freezer being turned hard against coarse Hawaiian rock salt.

I remember, too, the unforgettable sound of wailing mourners at Queen Lili'uokalani's funeral and the rustling of their regal black *holokus*.

And there was the sound of the shuffling of hundreds of shoes and the clapping of zoris as crowds of people squeezed together in an impromptu parade down Bishop and Fort Streets to noisily climb the two flights of stairs to the piers on Boat Day.

On the dock the sounds and smells mingled in tight embrace... the perfume of thousands of frangipani, carnations, jasmine, tuberose, and maile leis—many already being thrown overboard so the wearer would, for sure, return.

Today, occasional cruise ships try to imitate but fail. The streamers never reach the shore—the falsettos have vanished, and the monied cruisers continue on to spend just a few hours at another tropical port.

Arrivals have shifted to the airport, where visitors as well as jet-lagged islanders disembark like zombied wound-up computer aliens, laden with cocktails and free wine. They hurry past tour signs into escalators, crowded buses, and more waiting tour buses to see the newest State.

Meanwhile, in the mountains, there is the sound of wind moaning through the clustered needles of an ironwood tree, believed by some to be a demon in legend.

Smells

I could always tell when the wash woman was working by the pungent smell of her heavy, charcoal-loaded iron. She would glide the iron over the wrinkles, making them disappear, and wrap the starched dresses in Japanese newspaper.

Through the window would come the scent of wood smoke from the smoldering cinders beneath a Japanese *furo* (bath) that the *kane* (man) of the house was soaking in after a back-breaking day cutting sugar cane in the hot sun.

The first time I smelled the exotic aroma of curry, the popular mixture of spices from India, was in our school cafeteria, where it was used abundantly to flavor every beef, mutton, chicken, and fish stew in the daily plate lunch, which sold, of course, for a nickel. Even the wooden cigar box used to collect our lunch money smelled of curry. We barefoot kids did kitchen duty once a month, flirting with our gangling beaux as we peeled potatoes and carrots for stew, sliced tomatoes for salad, and washed greasy pots, pans, and dishes by hand with bar soap, and even that had curry smeared all over it! The slippery-sided tin sink reeked of stale curry and never drained properly. Today hot lunches at the old school are catered in for 75 cents.

And then there was the musky, murky smell of the basement lavatory at Lili'uokalani School, where water was always dripping on the wet, slippery floor, muddy from feet tramping back and forth.

Every time we went down to the old Uluniu Women's Swimming Club next to the Royal Hawaiian Hotel, there was the Oriental aroma of sukiyaki cooking on Japanese hibachis on table tops.

At home there were the kitchen smells, the tempting bouquet of stewed guavas as they were sieved through cheesecloth and left to drip all night long for homemade jams, jellies, and sherbet. We used fresh wild guavas picked during our mountain hikes. And when we drove on the two-lane dirt roads to 'Ewa and Wai'anae, we would stop and pick the tiny wild tomatoes and *poha* (Pacific goose berries) alongside the road. These, too, would fill the kitchen with their unique tang, as my mother boiled them together with sugar for preserves.

One of my favorite things at a lu'au was the tantalizing smells: of scorched burlap sacks as the *imu* (earth oven) was opened and the hot coals removed from the *opu* (belly) of the suckling pig that fell apart with a cloud of aroma into tasty *kalua* pig; of almost overripe breadfruit with a flavor of bananas and pineapple or Italian chestnuts; of baked sweet potatoes dug out of the neighbors' gardens that morning.

Spring had its own smell, too—a honeyed crispness, when the pink shower blossoms hung like carnation leis from branches, signifying the impending arrival of school vacation.

But on those last days of class the room would fill with the heady, intense perfume of bunches of white ginger blossoms our Hawaiian classmates brought from Palolo Valley. We thrust the stems in our blue inkwells on our open-topped wooden desks in grammar school and watched the ink soak through the veins of the waxen white flowers to tint them like a Monet painting.

When the fleet was in port and Uncle Sam's sailors invaded the town, there came the overwhelmingly clean smell of their uniforms. It was like flakes of Ivory soap had caught in the tightly creased, spotless white middies and tight-fitting bell-bottom trousers.

With the construction boom came the biting fragrance of tar on the new roads and the taste of it when we pulled pieces off the edges of the scalding-hot tar bins.

In neighbors' homes we might be tantalized by the odors of freshly baked loaves of soda bread made by our Irish friend, with lots of raisins and a sourdough flavor that permeated the kitchen. We bartered chickens for those loaves of bread. Or we would relish the smell of scones made by our Scottish friend, until we could eat them still hot from the oven.

My father, the chemist, allowed us to use chloroform to dope squirming centipedes with poison pincers on their mouths and scorpions with lethal stinging tails. The sickly sweet chloroform odor jumped from the bottles when we opened them. We removed the poisonous pincers of the centipedes and scorpions and let the drugged critters crawl all over our arms and legs, and in macabre childish glee we would scare the passersby walking up our lane on their way to board the trolley to town!

The mothers of two of my classmates developed leprosy. The women had exceedingly pink cheeks and palms. Before they were sent off to desolate Moloka'i, their houses emanated an oversweet ether-like smell. In those days there was no treatment nor hope of arresting the dreaded disease and a stigma existed, so all of us kept secret what we knew of those unfortunate families. How sad that the patients were torn from their loved ones and banished to the Moloka'i leprosy colony on the "unfriendly" isle forty miles from their homes on O'ahu. Today there is a drug to arrest the disease.

The air on the beach at Waikiki always seemed to waft rancid coconut oil, which the *wahine* (women) brushed into their luxuriant waist-length hair, and the beachboys lathered over their bodies. Sometimes those beachboys would use more of the oil to *lomi-lomi* (massage) the *wahine* tourists.

When you hiked mountain trails and slid downhill on ti leaves that shredded fast, there would come into your nostrils the dank organic presence of the rain forest. After a sudden rainstorm in the mountains, the cloud-fed waterfalls plunged steeply down sheer cliffs and steam rose from the ground below, as though the jungle were speaking in a rising earth voice, and the parched soil smelled at once of quenched thirst, if that has a smell.

As we sailed between the islands, we slept on deck overnight with a full moon overhead and listened to the soft strumming of guitars and 'ukuleles and singing of island songs by the *paniolo* (cowboys). Unfortunately, the stench of defecating cattle, which were loaded into the hold, couldn't be avoided. When the poor beasts made their way to the ships without benefit of docks, they had to be hauled into the water by the *paniolo* and swum out with ropes around their heads, their eyes bulging wide open, and scared to death!

Legends We Learned

From the time I was 3 years old and wandered down the hill to play with my Hawaiian friends, I listened to the stories their *kupuna* told of the strange occurrences in nature in old Hawai'i. And I have believed them ever since.

We have not a man in the moon, but a woman—Hina, a goddess of the sea who kept the moon in a special calabash hidden in the coral beds. She let it escape to the heavens on certain days for all to see. Hawaiians had a lunar calendar. Plantings were done and *makahiki* or feasting celebrations were held according to the phases of the moon.

When Hina was captured by the prince of the land, she mourned for her moon. When it was brought to her, she tried to run away to the heavens on the arch of the rainbow, but was pulled back by her jealous husband. She escaped and sailed with the moon high into the sky, where she reigns today, drying tapa, and crippled with an injured ankle.

Pele, goddess of the Big Island volcano, has always been a real being to me, especially when I spent a memorable evening with Hawaiian friends during the eruption that sent a river of lava over the village of Kapoho in 1960. A hedge of fire 1,500 feet high shot up in the cane fields and obliterated a school, the only American school ever destroyed by a lava flow.

Pele, like an enraged lover, was often jealous of her sister, Hi'iaka, who stole her lover. Pele appears in the lava flames with long flowing hair and eyes glowing like bits of volcanic glass. Sometimes she displays the slender, agile body of a young girl, although she also is often seen as a mongrel dog.

Moe Moe, the sleepyhead Rip Van Winkle of Hawai'i, is one of my favorite characters. He fell asleep so soundly that he was unaware of the *kukui* nut that rolled into his nostril and grew into a huge tree. Years later he was awakened when the tree was swaying in the wind. He magically extricated himself from the tree and returned to his family, an old man with a white beard.

Maui is the demigod who fished up our islands; today his fishhook can be seen in the constellation of Scorpio, with the eye as the giant red star, Antares. Maui discovered the *'alae* birds making fire and learned their secret, and won the gratitude of his people by teaching them how to make fire. He also snared the 16 legs of the sun in Haleakala "House of the Sun" crater on Maui, to make it go more slowly, thus allowing more sunny hours for drying tapa cloth. He pushed the sky up high so people could have more air to breathe, and used his kite to predict good weather, and originated sailing. He rescued his mother from the fierce *mo'omo'o* dragon, and died trying to steal the secret of everlasting life from Hina of the Night. If folks doubt his presence, they can look up into the heavens and see his stars of magic glowing in the shape of his fishhook.

When we hiked to Sacred Falls, we always placed a stone on a leaf in reverence for Kamapua'a, the Hog God, who saved his people by letting them climb out of the valley on the spines of his giant back and avert their pursuing enemy.

And, of course, we learned of the enchanting *menehune*, the small brown "little people" of Hawai'i who magically finished canoes by night, helped people fish, and delighted children with their whimsy. They, we know for sure, still live in the blue-eyed blossoms of *honohono* grass way up in cool valleys.

Rainy Day Rituals

It was always exciting to sail our paper boats in the rushing streams on our lane during the heavy rains of "winter." We made the boats by folding sheets of paper and turning corners the way Dad had taught us. Sometimes we even put baby lizards inside the tiny vessels. They never seemed afraid because their tails never came off.

We spent hours indoors during the rain, making all sorts of things, as we didn't have TV or even a radio then. We made paper beads for necklaces out of heavy, slick magazine paper, cutting out diamond shapes and rolling them up tight and brushing clear lacquer over them. When dry, they looked like porcelain beads, and we strung them for Christmas presents.

We made long garlands of fluffy white and yellow popcorn, which we exploded in a wire sieve basket over the gas burners. Or we strung leis of fresh, raw red cranberries for the Christmas tree. We made all of our Christmas ornaments: strings of cutouts that we colored—little dancing girls or clowns—or chains of colored strips of paper that locked into each other. We also lit dangerous candles attached with metal clips to the boughs of our brittle fir Christmas trees.

Another pastime was making paper dolls with complete wardrobes of rompers and "Cute Cuts" for play and, for parties, special ruffled dresses and shiny black patent leather or white Mary Jane shoes with straps across the tops.

We sewed all the clothes for our dolls from the dressmaker's scraps, even adding hand-stitched lace edges on knee-length panties that buttoned at the back, and camisoles atop bosoms with built-in ruffles for the rounded figure of the day.

Hair ribbons were other creations, made out of translucent-thin colored tissue paper. We affixed big bows to little heads with brass metal clasps, ready to match all outfits. Later we used brightly colored lacquer to dye our shoes to match the hair bows. The shoes often had two or three layers of paint, beginning to crack, applied by tiny hands on rainy days.

"Jump dot squares" was another rainy-day festivity, sort of a child's chess, where each turn gave you the privilege of filling in only one square, unless you completed a box. The winner had the most completed squares.

"The boy who lost his goose" was a cartoon Dad showed us from his teaching days in a one-room schoolhouse in California. We drew a cartoon to find the lost goose. We learned it and taught it to children and grandchildren.

When we tired of all of the above, we could bake oatmeal cookies or make shortbread, which took hours to do in those days with no mixes from the freezer that you simply cut up and popped in the oven. Making gingerbread men was another pastime, especially decorating them with raisins and nuts for eyes, noses, and buttons.

And when it rained in torrents, it was not unusual to see fashionably dressed secretaries and female lawyers kick off their stylish high-heeled pumps and peel off their hose to tiptoe barefoot across flooding streets to work, shoes under arms to keep them dry for the office. Even today the ladies do the same things, only it is more difficult to discard panty hose and scurry beneath 40-story high-rises!

Folks thought wearing shoes in the rain wasn't healthy anyway, because you might get mildewed, wrinkled feet. Of course, our fingers got crinkly when we swam in the ocean all day! So after we grew to adults, when it rained hard, the shoes came off with the hose and we carried them beneath an umbrella as we crossed the street barefoot!

When my boys attended grade school in California, they were always being sent to the principal's office, reprimanded for taking off their shoes. They'd arrive home with shoes over their shoulders, pouting because they had to wear shoes "even if it isn't raining."

Grammar School

The most memorable event in grade school was daily inspection of hands and hair, the latter for *uku* or head lice, or, in the case of the boys, ringworm.

Our strict Scottish first-grade teacher would walk up and down the narrow wooden aisles, bend over our outstretched hands like a Gestapo officer, flick her neatly manicured hands over our fingernails, and then weave her fingertips through bushy hair that she suspected had live bugs crawling in it. The girls with *uku* were yanked from their bench seats and sent to the principal, who poured kerosene on their heads and wrapped towels around them, so everyone at school knew exactly who had the *uku*. Ringworm victims got shaved heads and mercurochrome painted on them.

The teacher usually just patted me on top of my flat Dutch bob and smiled. I can't tell you how much I wished I'd had more hair like the girl in front of me with the kinky auburn mass of sun-scorched tresses (*uku* excepted). Later one day at recess in the dank, cement, basement lavatory, the girl with the toweled head shoved me into a corner and pushed me around, threatening me with: "Mebbe the teacha no look good you hair, she find *uku* awready!"

We learned reading and spelling from big phonetic charts with colorful lacquered pull-down sheets, and we chanted the sounds in unison—"ca-at, ra-at, th-uh, th-ay, who-wen, wa-tah!"

We had spelling bees and got high grades if we had good memories and could remember anything learned by rote and digested "by heart." I had a photographic memory. Anything I learned went in one ear long enough to get a high quiz grade, and went out the next day to oblivion.

Few of us in a class of 40 came from English-speaking homes. This situation led to the so-called English Standard schools in 1925, where those from foreign homes were weeded out by oral exams and we were speeded on without time wasted learning to speak English correctly. No longer necessary, as today students from multilingual homes speak English as well as pidgin, me included, "brah."

Our (Queen) Lili'uokalani school was a huge, imposing, two-story concrete building with large Grecian columns, very unlike architecture in the tropics. The only thing Hawaiian about it was its name, honoring the last queen of Hawai'i. We had to learn to sing "Aloha Oe" and "Hawai'i Pono'i", our island anthem, with all the correct Hawaiian words, or we weren't promoted to the next grade.

Today my old grammar school has been replaced by a tropical wooden two-story building.

We had a 14 year old boy with a mustache in our fourth grade, always being hauled out by reform school officers, who disrupted our class by marching in, Gestapo style, to take him out.

Today he would be given special help to keep him with classmates his age.

Our singing teacher was a lovable, plump Hawaiian lady who always smiled and wore a full-length *mu'umu'u* to contain her voluminous figure. She also taught us a few chords on the 'ukulele.

We had to learn how to plait (we always said "weave") with *lauhala*, leaves of the pandanus or *hala* tree, and make coasters and napkin rings with neatly turned corners. We gathered the long, dry, brown leaves below the *hala* trees in the neighborhood or at the beach, and soaked the leaves for several hours in salt water to soften them up, then stripped off the thorny edges, cut them into weaving strips, and wound them up neatly, ready for weaving.

The scent of white ginger still haunts me from that first school. We'd put the stems of the flowers in our blue inkwells atop our desks and watch the blossoms turn into new creations with indigo veins or into red ink to see bright scarlet emerge. And if we wanted purple streaks, we'd dip the flowers into both inks.

We were graded in "Deportment"—behavior—and I usually got a "D" because the teacher said that I talked too much. One time I was simply telling a classmate where she had dropped her pencil and I was given ten stinging whacks on my open palm for "talking." Appended to my report card was a postscript which read: "Margaret has yet to learn the lesson of 'M.Y.O.B.' (mind your own business)!

I later attended Aliʻiolani school down Waiʻalae Avenue, Hawaiʻi's first English Standard school, erected on half of Bell's Dairy near Palolo Valley. Mrs. Bell wouldn't give up her land and delighted in letting her fierce bull loose during our recess. We literally had to run for our lives to classrooms and shut the windows.

We had wonderful explorations to Palolo Stream before school to catch swordtail guppies for our classroom aquarium and green frogs, which we'd hide in our desks and let loose behind the teacher's back.

Graduation from the eighth grade was a big event, with a printed program, valedictorian, and baskets of fresh flowers given the new girl graduates instead of the leis they wear today. Girls wore special white organdy dresses and the boys donned ties with their short-sleeved white shirts. And for the occasion we all bought shoes that pinched our "luʻau feet!"

How vividly I remember not roller-skating home up Waiʻalae Avenue the day I "became a woman," but boarding the open streetcar for the occasion. I held my head high and suspected everyone was looking at me and noticing that I was different, that memorable day in my 12th year.

The way we learned:

Penmanship: The Palmer method with large, sweeping circles counterclockwise. (Today 'twould be called Pen-*person*-ship?) We began with the right hand going in orbits above the paper. We made letters leaning starboard so that the bottom of the letter rested gently on the bottom line of the special penmanship notebook and the top reached two spaces above. The writing was boringly uniform, with no trace of the personality of the penman. Today if one knows he or she is going to be anyone who fills out a prescription, heads a museum (e.g. Donald Duckworth), bank, or fund raiser, they should skip pen-person-ship entirely and concentrate on Chinese hieroglyphics.

Brushing Teeth: Almost the same arm movement and direction of above, except that brushes went *across* the teeth in our day, not up and down from the gums. Plain old inexpensive salt was also suggested for rubbing on with fingers like we did at Girl Scout camp when we forgot our brushes. Today salt is a no-no and considered bad to ingest, so one can use baking soda paste made by diluting with hydrogen peroxide (cheaper than today's toothpastes). After I purchased an electric toothbrush and water pick as an adult, my new dentist said it was safer and more efficient to use a child's soft toothbrush to reach corners in the back! Now another electric device is recommended! It was simpler in the old days.

Health: Cleanliness was godliness when we were young, and we took baths, changed clothes daily, especially socks, if worn. We ironed skirts and dresses, when girls wore them and not slacks. Today rock performers on music videos are unshaven, unwashed, hair knotted in snarls, exhibiting tattoos, and wearing "shades" to cover bloodshot eyes from too much booze and dope. Smellier is better, they say.

Sex Education: Old days, zero! Today they tell you on TV of bargains at the drug store for condoms in a variety of colors, or anti-sperm sponges distributed by some schools without parents' consent. Virginity is on the decline.

Sex Education in our family was to the point. When we started dating in our late teens, my Victorian mother had one line of cautious advice:

"Girls, remember this—don't let a boy kiss you more than once—it isn't good."

Well, I tried it and it was *very* good!

Physical Education: Today it means sophisticated and costly equipment with gym workout areas, special jogging, basketball, baseball, and football shoes and socks, jerseys and pants so tight one cannot afford to sneeze. Tennis culottes display sexy thighs and swimsuits bare behinds. Our games were free and we wore clothes from our cupboards.

Geography: Memorizing capitals of countries throughout the world that we could never locate on the globe. Today students listen to TV news as it happens and, before learning about a country, watch on the screen to see if it still exists; e.g. the Soviet Union, East Germany, Yugoslavia.

Arithmetic: We sang in rote: "2+2=4" or "2x2=4" and prizes were given for adding up sums on the blackboard faster than the guy before you. Today kids do it all with computers and have more fun.

Schools for Learning?: Our discipline lessons learned in grade school, plus the "3 Rs," were preparation for adulthood, we were told. Today kids gang up for street riots to prove to peers they are tough and ready for fights, and for jail to come (how did jails come to be called "correctional facilities"?). With no parental supervision, the kids still grow up. Mother is working to help pay off the house mortgage, car, and furniture monthly allotments. And single mothers live off welfare the best they can. Oh, for those simple, predictable, unstressed days of my youth.

Eats

We made homemade ice cream or sherbet of soursop and papayas we grew, guavas we picked growing wild, or pineapples we picked in the fields after the commercial harvest. Everyone had a turn at cranking the old wooden bucket packed with chunks of ice and hard rock salt, and at licking the metal blades when the delicious dessert was ready for storing in the coldest part of the old icebox.

Often we stopped at the ice cream parlor for Sunday supper of just ice cream and fresh fruit on top.

Panini, or prickly pear fruit, tasted like overly sweet mushy watermelon and was best ice-cold and carefully eaten with the fin-

A poi luncheon at Kahala beach with me, second from the right, yawning like a "howler" monkey, 1919.

gers, after peeling with a knife and fork. You knocked the fruit off the cactus plant with sticks, very cautious not to let any of the fine, hairy spines get near your skin.

A kid's cookout consisted of burning leaves (permissible then), into which we threw raw potatoes that got black on the outside. We ate them mashed up with canned evaporated milk, butter, and salt.

We never had to pay for commercial lu'aus as Oriental feasts were given by our friends when babies were a year old or when folks got married. Receptions were held under canopies with island music and hula dancing, a festive time for all from *kupuna* (grandparents or aunties) to the new babies.

I never had a problem downing poi, as I never thought it tasted like library paste (plain flour and water in our day), as many tourists believed it did. I never made a grimace of displeasure because I learned to eat it with my little fingers as a child at my Hawaiian friends' homes, even though the only way my mainland-bred parents could stand it was with sugar and milk, offered that way to tourists today as a "poi cocktail."

During the second World War, babies were fed a tasty cereal made from taro, sucrose, and milk, called "taro lactum." Their parents took tins of it with them to the mainland.

Homemade goodies were made from scratch with no mixes available. Healthy oatmeal and raisin cookies, paper-thin crisp sugar wafers, shortbread and scones from our Scottish friends from South Africa, sponge cakes cut in half and served with fresh whipped cream flavored with real vanilla, German *ameritter* (French toast), Swedish and brown rice pancakes with real maple syrup, and tins of cookies sent overseas during both wars were some of our old-time treats.

We made rice, dry Oriental style, in our fireless cooker that had metal dishes heated over the stove and put below large metal pots with tight-fitted covers. The rice cooked there slowly for an hour and we could use the closed cooker as a bench for sitting in the kitchen. We took our rice and stew in these containers to the beach for supper.

Folks grew Isabella grapes on trellis vines in home gardens. The sweet slip-skin grapes made excellent preserves. Vineyard Boulevard was named after these grapes, no longer grown here because folks prefer the sweet, seedless table grapes we get today from California and Chile.

The Street Car

The highlight of my entire childhood in Kaimuki was the open-sided electric streetcar. The tracks ended up our hill at the corner of Wai'alae and Koko Head Avenues. After seven decades, I can still hear it clanging and careening down the hill to town (Honolulu) or with a transfer to Waikiki or Manoa Valley.

I used to help the conductor turn the wooden bench seats forward and watch him crank the overhead sign to read "Honolulu," or take his motor car gear from the counter in back to the forward driving area.

The car was open on both sides and featured wide running boards and perpendicular bars to hold on to, like riding a merry-go-round or San Francisco's cable cars. There were also thick metal cow-catcher bumpers fore and aft.

One windy day when the streetcar was crossing Mo'ili'ili stream, (now the entrance to the H1 Freeway past the University of Hawai'i), my insecure pink hair ribbon blew off into the water below. The friendly conductor, who knew everyone on his car from Kaimuki to town, stopped the car and shouted:

"Eh, you folks, go look Margaret's hair ribbon, yeah?"

"In the watta ovah there!"

And with that directive, practically all the concerned passengers slid off their comfortable dry seats and literally plunged down the muddy red dirt bank to the rushing stream below. And came up with my soggy pink hair bow a little worse for wear!

I used to dream about running that car and knew every twist and turn of the motorman's hand as he swung into gear. The engine made these sounds as it caught up steam: "Klonk, klonk, klonkety klonk, chuck-a-chuck" and finally a nice, easy "shssssh!" At the start of the route you could see all the way to town and the A'ala train station, straight down through an avenue of brightly colored hedges of red and pink hibiscus, oleander, palm trees, flowering pink and golden shower trees, flaming *poinciana regia*, monkeypods, and *kiawe*. In May, colorful red and white paper carp flying on bamboo poles for Boys' Day decorated the streets.

Later I climbed 4,000-foot Mt. Ka'ala, O'ahu's highest, and found soggy tree trunks with hanging moss and *'ape* leaves five feet across. The whole jungle looked like it should have had dinosaurs roaming through it, a weird place!

I was always intrigued by the Chinese man with the long pinkie fingernail who held his fare in his ear and deftly flicked it out with his nail at pay time.

I also liked to watch the kimono-clad Japanese ladies nursing their babies which they carried in slings over their bent backs.

Many Hawaiians wore hat leis of real pheasant feathers with golds or peacock blue, handed down from generation to generation, always an island identity. Once when I was wearing one in the bullfight arena of 80,000 in Mexico City, a man right behind me tapped me on the shoulder and asked in the pidgin way of dropping the end of a question (like the British): "You from da I-land?" And we discovered I was a classmate of his son in high school!

You heard all languages on the streetcar, seldom English, as most haole (whites) had cars; but, my dear mother, having smashed through our wooden garage wall twice, was prohibited from driving her little girls to town or the beach, by Father, who liked his Model T in one piece. "Take a cab, Rose." But I am glad she didn't.

Hawaiians spoke their guttural language. The Orientals chatted loudly in their sing-song tones, which always sounded like chimes to me. The Filipinos carried on in their soft words with many gestures. Lots of the younger Hawaiians played their 'ukuleles and sang as we rode along on the fascinating streetcar of my childhood.

How happy I was my mother never learned to drive!

My Waikiki

Going to Waikiki from our home in Kaimuki seemed like an all-day affair and took over an hour on two streetcars, with a transfer in between. We boarded the streetcar at the end of the Kaimuki line at the top of Wai'alae Avenue, where the conductors we all knew waited even ten minutes if they saw someone puffing up the hill a block away toward the trolley.

As folks sauntered up to the wide running boards open the length of the electric Rapid Transit, they visited with one another and exchanged news of the neighborhood. We all knew each other, even though most homes were a block apart in Kaimuki with its *kiawe* trees and lava outcroppings, a sparse settlement in the scrubby wild growth of tropical morning glory vines, bougainvillea, and panax and hibiscus hedges.

The end of the Kaimuki line was the beginning to town and Waikiki. We'd lug along a huge pot of homemade stew in our fireless cooker container and carefully balance it between our bare feet beneath the seats, as things could slide right off the open-sided electric streetcar when it careened down the steep hill on the big trip to Waikiki. It was as exciting as riding the San Francisco cable cars, and quite a bit like it those days.

McCully corner at King Street was the transfer point for Waikiki, and did we love it! We'd stop at the old Chinese store that had huge glass jars of crackseed and, when my mother wasn't looking, we kids would buy a whole nickel bag. By the time the Waikiki trolley arrived from town, the thin paper transfer slip we clutched was pretty gooey as we handed it to the new conductor.

It was like entering a real jungle for kids those days in Waikiki. The avenue down Kalakaua to the end of the line at Kapi'olani Park, the zoo, and the aquarium was lined with coco palms and hid the only hotel, the regal, white Moana. Date palms and tamarind trees hung over carpets of heavy pollen on the ponds. An arcade of thick ironwood trees stood as a windbreak from the zoo to Diamond Head. The Rapid Transit Company built the aquarium so folks would ride to the end of the line.

A lazy stream cut through the boundary of the Moana Hotel from the Seaside bungalows across the street, where the International Market Place stands today.

We played Tarzan tag in the huge tangled canopy of *hau* trees that encircled Waikiki Bay. We crawled in the gnarled mass like monkeys in an almost impenetrable labyrinth, without touching the ground. The last kid to remain in the arbor was the winner.

We belonged to the original Outrigger Canoe Club alongside the Moana Hotel, which cost $10 a year dues for the entire family and six free guests a month. You brought your chow and warmed it up on the gas stove in the small community kitchen. Often Olympic swim champ Duke Kahanamoku and several beachboys shared supper with us.

The focal point of the club in those days was not any cocktail bar or restaurant but the sand volleyball court in front of the old green wooden dressing rooms on the street side. We kids lined up on the sides and watched as the teams of husky surfers grunted in Hawaiian as they played.

Waikiki Beach, 1920s. Hawaii State Archives, Eaton Magoon Collection.

We'd watch the beachboys drag out their huge canoes from beachside stalls for paying guests and often get free rides as they were warming up. We listened to them play 'ukuleles and guitars and sing as they sat in the cool sand between the canoe berths. It was really like belonging to a club of all the old-timers in Honolulu. Islanders dominated the beaches in those days with very few tourists.

Well known around the club besides Duke were lady Olympic stars Mariechen Weshlau and Helen Moses, and the great swimmer Buster Crabbe, who later played Tarzan and Flash Gordon in the movies.

There was also the legendary petite and frail Grandma Waters, who had been shipped to Hawai'i from Boston to die of some ailment in 1916. Instead, she learned to surf at 67 on a special board built by her son, Ted. She gave philosophical advice to youngsters in her raspy voice and lived to 100 in spite of a broken hip; and she was alert to the last.

In 1930 her son, Ted Waters, designed and made the first hollow surfboard out of pine and redwood, and later a balsa board, no longer used for today's acrobatics on small fiberglass boards.

I learned how to pick the right kind of *limu* (seaweed) to eat on the coral reef off Waikiki, and I chewed it as I swam or rode with a beachboy on his large surfboard, and sometimes on his shoulders. I also learned to speak pidgin along with the beachboys, but got soap in my mouth if my parents heard it!

We girls challenged one another in the lethal game of Sunburn. The winner was the one to have the most blistered skin to peel off her back the next day. It came off in sheets of crisp skin with a bright-red, almost bleeding, layer beneath. It hurt so much we couldn't even stand a sheet over us that night! Sometimes we soaked in a tea bath, but the injury had been done. No one ever heard of sunscreen then; and coconut oil, which basted you more, was a later innovation. We never lay in the sun just to get a tan, but swam from morning 'til lunchtime, with an hour out for a nap, and then in again till supper time. This we did at least three times a week and usually daily, if we had a summer cottage on the ocean. And we all got virulent cases of skin cancer later in life—an accumulation of too much sun!

By law all men had to cover their chests and so they wore tank tops and shorts or one-piece woolen suits that were scratchy and took forever to dry. *Haole* ladies wore knee-length, black sateen cotton bloomers and elbow-length blouses with long, black cotton stockings, bathing caps and rubber bathing shoes. Hawaiian women and girls usually swam in their mu'umu'us and let the salt water soak in their thick, wavy hair.

Canoe rides back then were 50 cents each for Outrigger Club members and $1 for others, for three waves from a mile out to shore. Moonlight trips were $2 and surfboard lessons $3 an hour.

I remember seeing Mary Pickford and husband, Doug Fairbanks, Sr., on the beach at Waikiki. Everybody who was a celebrity came to Waikiki and stayed at the Moana, and later the Royal Hawaiian, which we watched go up next to our club.

There was always nostalgia when folks honeymooned at Waikiki and strolled to the gazebo end of the romantic pier of the Moana Hotel and were serenaded by the beachboys.

We later joined the Uluniu Women's Swimming Club adjacent to the Royal. We relished the delicious *hekka* or sukiyaki dinners for 75 cents apiece. The cooks wore kimonos and cooked the feast on a charcoal brazier at the table, which was set with blue-and-white-patterned Nikko design china.

At age 10 my best friend was a smiling *hapa haole* girl whose parents were both half Hawaiian and whose modest, bright coral-pink bungalow home was in the heart of Waikiki. A full length outrigger canoe was under the shade of a tall mango tree next to a Model T Ford, only a block from the rolling surf at Waikiki. Their bent-over, smiling, toothless Japanese cook prepared platters of fresh fish caught by one of my friend's brothers, who fished with a spear and throw net and caught enough for their entire family of eight kids. He also composed many popular island songs, played the guitar, and sang in the evenings at Waikiki hotels.

Their stately Hawaiian-Scottish mother always wore a long, colorful *holomu'u* and a tortoise-shell comb in her thick, upswept coiffure. Their fair, blue-eyed Hawaiian-Swedish father was always meticulously attired in a white Palm Beach suit and Panama hat with a feather lei. I can see him yet, smoking a large cigar on his front verandah, as he rocked in his chair and hummed a song.

Their friends spoke Hawaiian and everybody would sing at any time of day and feast at the tables laden with ti leaves, poi, *limu* (seaweed), pork, chicken, and lu'au, always set as though company were expected. As soon as the *kaukau* was consumed, the cook brought in more full platters of food and pink and lemon sodas for the kids. Real Hawaiian tapa and hand-sewn quilts covered four-poster beds, where we young ones were often put down for naps in between hula entertainment by the family members.

It was at this welcome home that I learned the Hawaiian words to the old songs, to play the 'ukulele and sing, and to dance the hula. And I continued to eat every morsel of squid, eel, fish, and poi with relish! It was here that I played the piano and sang duet in the wedding song, "Ke Kali Nei Au," when my friend was married in the tiny "parlor," as it was always called by her mother and father. The room had a frieze done in brightly colored oils, painted by family members, which depicted seascapes and Pele's eruptions.

Me, at age 3 in 1917, at Waikiki beach with my dad.

Learning to paddle at the beach in 1919, where the Kahala Mandarin Oriental now stands.

Another fun place was the Castle mansion at the Diamond Head end of Waikiki. The building later became the first Elks Club. It had gleaming Austrian chandeliers and a huge French mirror at the foot of the three-story spiral stairwell. Shiny, slippery mahogany railings guarded the stairs, and oh how we delighted in sliding down those railings! The sea in front of the mansion was rougher than central Waikiki and rushed between the pilings beneath the building. We had great fun bodysurfing there. Formal evening balls were held on the premises for the older folks, and we often got to stay for part of the evening if we put on pretty dresses and uncomfortable Mary Jane shoes.

We swam in the new Waikiki Natatorium Olympic-size swimming pool with buoyant salt water, a memorial to those who served in World War I. We had our junior high meets there at night, and I remember how cold and hard the tiered cement bleacher seats were when the wind picked up, and how freezing when we came out wet and had to wait for the final relay team event. (In Hawai'i, anything under 70 degrees is "freezing.")

Our Waikiki extended around the lighthouse, with church picnics on an estate next to what became Doris Duke's Grecian palace. Where the Kahala Mandarin Oriental now stands, I learned to surf with the small board my dad made me.

The night lights at Waikiki were mellow Japanese lanterns strung along the waterfront hotels, and fluttering torches of the fishermen in low tide offshore, casting mysterious shadows on the foamy white surf. The waves pulsed as a muted bass backdrop to soft string music and the haunting tremolo of steel guitars and falsetto voices.

Years later Waikiki Beach was my beat as a reporter for the dailies. I interviewed movie stars, musicians, and politicians, VIPs on the big white ships coming and going from all over the world. And the stories were fabulous. That was 1936, the heyday of the steamship liners coming to Hawai'i.

Movie stars put on an act of arriving in the Islands by ship. Reporters went offshore in a small launch to meet the ships off Waikiki. First, you had to find the elusive stars, interview and photograph them, and dash back to the Merchant Street press before deadline at 10 a.m., composing the lead of your story in your head along the way. As you typed out the opening paragraphs, folks were still unloading at the pier.

I spent the first day of Fred McMurray's honeymoon with him and his bride. They stayed at the Halekulani. They wanted seclusion and guidance on what to see, and asked me to show them in their chauffeured convertible!

Bette Davis had a three-way telephone hookup to retape the audio for her new movie. We found her jumping up and down on her bed in white tennis shorts, nervously puffing on a cigarette. The director was in Hollywood, Bette at the Royal here, and her leading man, Charles Boyer, in New York.

As cameras were poised and everyone hushed for voices from afar, Boyer began with "Darling, I love you ..." and Bette screamed, "My God, Charles, shut up! You've got the wrong script!" And it began all over again, making a better story, of course.

Comedian Frank Morgan (usually drunk), broke up the lobby crowd at the Royal one night as he really saw double—a pair of twins registered at the hotel—and reeled by, shouting, "Gad, there are two, I swear!"

Bing Crosby rode his moped (in the days of limousines for stars) from his fancy rented Diamond Head home to play volleyball with the beachboys at the Outrigger. He arrived bare chested, breaking the "decency law."

Jeannette MacDonald threatened to leave the Royal unless the myna birds stopped waking her up in the morning. Although all kinds of tests were conducted, none helped. The birds would not budge and would not shut up, and neither would Jeannette MacDonald.

Beachboys

Hawai'i's famous beachboys at Waikiki have been making visitors' stays in the Islands memorable since the turn of the century.

The favorite spot for spooners was the romantic out-over-the-water gazebo at the end of the old wooden pier of the Moana Hotel, where beachboys serenaded the couples in the moonlight.

When the ships arrived, the musicians would also come to homes uptown in the valleys, or Kaimuki and Kahala, and entertain guests the evening of their arrival. The music was soft and sweet, often sung in falsetto, and everyone relaxed on the lawns or sat on the lanai, with leis draped everywhere. There was an overwhelming fragrance of heavily scented tropical flowers—plumerias, gardenias, carnations, *pikake*, tuberoses, and spicy *maile* from the Big Island forests.

Beachboys in the twenties and thirties were usually native Hawaiians, who earned what money they could in taking visitors for outrigger canoe rides, giving surfing lessons, teaching swimming, playing music in the afternoons and evenings, and giving *lomi* or Hawaiian massage. They even cared for children of clients for pay and extra tips, which could be lucrative in those days, and some went back on the luxury liners with wealthy widows as traveling companions.

The beachboy did not watch a clock for pay. Usually he was attached to a group, and later beach concessions at various Waikiki hotels, and he got a percentage of the cost of the rides he gave tourists. He was endowed with natural charm and spent a happy time making others happy, having fun relaxing at Waikiki.

The old surfboards were 15 to 16 feet long and weighed

Hawaiian beachboys in 1926, Waikiki, with Duke Kahanamoku fifth from the right. Bishop Museum, used with permission from the Outrigger Duke Kahanamoku Foundation

120 to 130 pounds. Beachboys lifted them with ease and carried them on their muscled shoulders, but haoles usually hauled the boards to the water's edge with boat trailers. In the thirties, the boards were made of hollow redwood with a metal screw valve on top to let water out after a surf. These were dangerous if you "pearled" (allowed the nose of the board to go underwater), because then the surfboard would skyrocket out from under your feet, and when it came back down the screw could hit you in the head!

We knew every beachboy as a personal friend and hung around a few yards out for free rides in the outriggers before the paying tourists arrived and were seated.

There was Frank Teles, a part-American Indian, who loved chocolate cake so much he would bet teenage guests that he could perform a special feat, and if he lost he'd give free surfing lessons, and if he won they'd hand over a chocolate cake. The trick for Teles, then age 34 and a former AAU (Amateur Athletic Union) high-dive world champion, was to run and dive head first over a 4-foot spiked fence and land in the sand with a somersault 14 feet away! And he did, always!

Steamboat Bill, a lifeguard, lived 92 years and taught hundreds of folks how to paddle heavy canoes, to *lomi*, swim, and surf.

Panama Dave, a French Tahitian, got his name because he had no front teeth and he could spit out a full mouth of water through his teeth in a gushing stream "like the Panama Canal!"

Rabbit Kekai was really "Robert," but his friends pronounced it like "Rabbit." Chick Daniels was "some chick," and Splash Lyons made a big splash one time instead of a smooth dive. In his late seventies, Splash still entertained weekly at the new Elks Club with other old-time beachboys.

More of the gang that I knew were Curly Cornwall, Typhoon or Cyclone Spencer, Freckles Lyons, Sally Hale, one so big and strong he was just called Ox, and Hawkshaw Howell—with a face that looked like someone stuck his chin on lopsided as an afterthought, but famous for carrying beautiful gals on his shoulders in tandem surfing.

Hawai'i's beachboys formed their first official group, Hui Nalu, in 1912, under Dude Miller. By then the Moana Hotel was booming, and by 1929 the Royal Hawaiian, Halekulani, and Seaside hotels were filled with guests enjoying the

Outrigger Canoe Club, with the famous names of beachboys filling the memories of many tourists and islanders alike.

The Great Duke

One Sunday morning in the summer of 1911, three island boys were asked to race as they swam in the open sea at Sans Souci, Waikiki. Unbeknownst to the swimmers, one of the spectators pulled out a stopwatch and clocked them. All three boys had broken the world's records in the 50- and 100-yard freestyle!

The boys were Duke Kahanamoku and Curtis and Harold Hustace. None had ever trained or seen the inside of a swimming tank. The man who timed them was William T. Rawlins,

Duke Kahanamoku, left, riding a wave on his surfboard, 1912; Right, standing in front of his surfboard, 1913. Hawaii State Archives, used with permission from the Outrigger Duke Kahanamoku Foundation

an island lawyer from Yale University, whose belief that the beachboys swam faster than they knew was proven in a few seconds.

This was the start of Duke's career in four Olympic Games and other meets which took him to Stockholm, Antwerp, Hamburg, Paris, Australia, and New Zealand with acclaim from the world as Hawai'i's Ambassador of Goodwill!

The attorney Rawlins, Dude Miller, a beachboy, and Lew Henderson, a Pearl Harbor architect, helped the three swimmers form the Hui Nalu club in 1912, a few months before Hawai'i's first AAU meet was held off Pier 5 in Honolulu Harbor. The boys had to belong to a club in order to get official recognition for their swimming records. As they swam that August 12 between the coal barges in the open sea, Duke broke all existing freestyle records by a combined 10 seconds!

Word of Duke's sensational times in the 50-, 100-, and 220-yard freestyle events traveled like wildfire throughout the athletic world.

He was rushed to the mainland a few months after the island meet and for the first time had a coach, George Kistler of Australia, who trained the young man systematically in the University of Pennsylvania tank in Philadelphia.

It was a big day for Duke when he swam with the American team in the Olympics in Stockholm in 1912. He swam the 100-meter freestyle in less than 55 seconds, breaking the record and leaving the famous European champion Bretting holding the bag.

After his celebrated races in Germany, Duke swam in the Seine, and in the Olympics in Paris and Antwerp.

He broke more records later in three more Olympic Games in Europe, Australia, and New Zealand.

When asked how he felt about becoming a world champ, Duke modestly replied, "Well, I never realized I was that good. In fact, I thought if I ever got as far as San Francisco, I would have seen the world. I never dreamed that I would get into four Olympics and see Europe."

Duke smiled as he recalled the time he swam the 100-yard dash at the World's Fair in San Francisco in 1915. He was competing against Rathael of Chicago and they ended in a dead heat. After 15 minutes' rest, they went at it again and this time Duke beat him by a whole body length. Everyone went wild and someone pushed Harvey Chilton, the island coach, right into the tank with all his clothes on!

During the first World War, Duke toured the States, giving benefit performances for the Red Cross in exhibition swim meets.

Duke, who grew up in Kakaʻako, was the first son of nine children of the captain of the Honolulu police force. He was named "Duke" by his father after the Duke of Edinburgh. Duke's mother was the daughter of the High Chief of Kauaʻi. At Kamehameha School for Hawaiians, Duke learned the machinist's trade and blacksmithing and later took up commercial studies at McKinley High School.

A few days before his 50th birthday, Duke married (for the first time) a dancing teacher many years his junior. She had been carrying a torch for him since she was a child in Cincinnati, Ohio. She passed through Hawaiʻi with her parents as a kid when Duke began his swim meets here in 1912, and in high school had kept a scrapbook of news clips on him. I introduced them at the old Outrigger Club when she was my dance teacher at the Royal Hawaiian Hotel next door.

Duke's special surfboard was 12 feet long and weighed 70 pounds. It was designed especially for him out of balsa and redwood, hollow and laminated,

Duke Kahanamoku holding up high chief Paki's surfboard in the Bishop Museum Courtyard, 1957.
Bishop Museum, Honolulu Star-Bulletin, used with permission from the Outrigger Duke Kahanamoku Foundation

with no keel, which folks thought much too dangerous then. The board stands in the Bishop Museum today for all to see.

At 56, this well-built athlete, 6 feet one inch tall and weighing 220 pounds, was still the idol of thousands. He enjoyed sailing an S-boat off Diamond Head, spearing and casting a net for fish, playing long hours of volleyball at the Outrigger Canoe Club, and surfing and swimming in the ocean he loved. In 1933 he was elected sheriff, the first of eight consecutive terms. He greeted all the dignitaries who visited Hawai'i.

Sheriff Duke Kahanamoku.
Bishop Museum, used with permission from the Outrigger Duke Kahanamoku Foundation

"Swimming in the old days was certainly different from what it is today," Duke once reminisced. "We had no fancy swimming pools, no lanes marked off, no coaches and special training. We just swam out in the open sea, surfed, and enjoyed ourselves. Today swimmers have everything dished out to them on gold platters, and the Hawaiians don't seem to be taking advantage of the situation."

He was Waikiki's silent strong man, and the tales of his strength were told like legends. Like the time he single-handedly moved a 100-square-foot shed with a crowbar after an entire group of men couldn't budge it! And once he blithely lifted up the heavy front end of a mammoth canoe and held it aloft as four men strained to raise the stern from the slippery sand!

He stopped two sailors from fistfighting by grabbing both men simultaneously, one in each hand, and hoisting them high above his head, until they promised not to beat up each other anymore! And this, after breaking the 50-yard dash record at the nearby YMCA!

Years later at Waikiki I experienced one of my most poignant memories. I was there with hundreds of others to pay final tribute to my childhood friend, Duke Kahanamoku. He had died a revered old man, with hair as white as bleached coral and a kindly tanned face with soulful lines.

We stood on the shore break, where I had surfed with him at the site of the old Outrigger Canoe Club, now no more. A maze of high-rises hemmed in his beach. But the sea was still warm and restless and sent wavelets with scalloped edges on the sand endlessly, just as it was the first day Duke entered it from his childhood home nearby. He would enter it now for the last time.

We watched as his ashes were reverently placed in the canoe he loved. With misty eyes and trembling fingers, we placed our fragrant flowers upon the bow. So many leis and blossoms.

We watched in silence as the beachboys slid the sleek dugout into the emerald water and paddled through the surf beyond the reef to send Duke home into the sea he loved. The hot tropic sun shone brightly and the azure sea reflected the brilliance of the cloud-flecked sky, as though the heavens knew an *ali'i* (royalty) had arrived.

I was glad to have known him in the Waikiki of my youth.

Daisy Was Our Zoo

It would be years before I learned that a daisy wasn't an elephant. When I was growing up, the only Daisy I knew was my friend and everyone's favorite animal at the Kapi'olani Park zoo.

Every Sunday we got free rides on Daisy in the unfenced, unlandscaped zoo grounds that also contained Jenny the chimpanzee, and a few bears, leopards, monkeys, camels, and yawning lions, whose echoing roars were heard as far away as our home near the Kaimuki fire station.

We'd scamper up a huge banyan tree to board Daisy and slide down the gnarled trunks to reach her scratchy undulating broad back. She seemed to know all of us kids who rode her and would turn her huge head to peer at us with her small beady eyes and long lashes. For years we had fed her peanuts by hand, and once wI got a bloody finger where the needle-sharp hairs on her trunk pierced my hand. They poked like a painful *kiawe* thorn and there were plenty of those around to plague little bare feet.

The keeper would lead Daisy with a short rope leash on our magical trips, and she was always serene and happy to have us giggly kids aboard. We would pat her thick, crenulated back as she moved along quietly and slowly in the wild maze of date palms, tamarind trees, *kiawe,* and shady monkeypods. It seemed like Robinson Crusoe's island, that zoo of the twenties.

When we returned from our elephant ride, we would slip off her leathery back into the arms of her keeper and march along behind him like he was the Pied Piper; he led Daisy back to her sparse cement shelter, where she was chained to a post. The leash was so short she could hardly reach her hay pile or water trough beneath a heavy metal security bar.

Sometimes the keeper would also take us for a jaunt on a camel. We climbed a short ladder to the seats on either side

Riding Daisy, the African elephant, at the Honolulu Zoo, 1919. R. J. Baker, Bishop Museum

of the high back of the desert beast, and rocked along for another trip through our jungle. Afterwards we'd dust off warm thick dates from the ground and munch on them along with the succulent acidy fruit of the tamarind seed pods Mother liked to use for cold tea.

I remember when 3-year-old Daisy arrived in 1916 from Vancouver, Canada. Women and children aboard the ship had been riding her daily on deck and she was the darling one-ton pet of everyone. Daisy was welcomed to Hawai'i with a "Down in Jungle Town" parade. The city supervisor rode her with balloons tied to her head. A band followed along behind. On the way to the zoo she even stopped by the *Advertiser* newspaper office and lumbered inside to bid hello to the gang there.

Daisy came from Rhodesia in 1914 and was one of only twelve African elephants in captivity. The city paid $3,000 for her to start the new Honolulu Zoo, but never gave her a home where she could be comfortable.

Luckily she had a former circus trainer, George Conradt, as her keeper for 17 years. He got up every day at 2 a.m. at his nearby home to feed her and take her for a daily walk before chaining her to what was really an inhumane short leash in a small open hut. I'll never understand why Mr. Conradt, who loved her and seemed to understand her, would do that. There she stood for those 17 years, frustrated, often just rocking back and forth. As time went by, she went berserk from this cruel confinement. She became irritable, and finally one day in 1926 she broke her leash and ran amok.

We witnessed the entire rampage that fateful day. We were feeding her peanuts by hand when she wrenched free of her leg chain and walked over the security bar and headed for freedom. We looked up and she was practically on top of us as we stood there with peanuts in our hands. My usually calm mother lifted her long skirts and shouted: "Run, girls, run!" Frantically we scampered to the bushes in the adjacent open polo field and watched a sight I shall never forget.

Daisy romped like a crazed giant as she ran amok, her swirling trunk wildly tearing into the soft tops of cars, rolling the vehicles over as though they were medicine balls. She curled her trunk around full-grown coco palms like a boa constrictor and knocked them over and uprooted trees in all directions!

Finally someone roused her sleeping keeper and he calmed her down, but poor Daisy was then put on a shorter chain leash and no longer could we ride our pet. She was considered too dangerous.

In 1933, the city was about to execute her because the Humane Society urged officials either to kill her or build her better quarters. She had been given a 60-day stay in her death sentence while the city tried to scrape up $8,000 for her new home. Seattle Zoo even promised to donate a baby elephant as a new playmate. Ironically, the city planners were approving funds for her new spacious home when she went berserk again.

Her keeper had just resigned at 69 and the city was looking for a new one. Onlookers called him from home to subdue her. He arrived and walked slowly to her and seemed to calm her. She even caressed him as he led her back to her chained leash. But just before they reached it, Daisy turned on Mr. Conradt and knocked him down with her trunk, then stomped on him, instantly killing her best friend. Police found her quietly standing over him under a tree, not resisting being shot. They fired several bullets into her head with .30 caliber Army rifles.

How sad for our Daisy.

The town was devastated by her death, as though an old friend had passed on. Hundreds of folks rushed to the zoo to see her four-ton body lying in a muddy pool of blood, and everyone wept. Her body was buried four miles out at sea.

My dad's home movies of her in happier days with us on her back were shown at the central downtown drugstore, Benson Smith's, at the corner of Fort and Hotel Streets. It was a neat old community drugstore, where everyone gathered for sodas and chitchat.

In the Rice Paddies With Popo

Visits to the fascinating, petite Chinese grandma of our live-in family helper were special memories of my childhood. The magical old woman lived in a wooden hut on stilts above the rice paddies on Kalakaua Avenue, just below King Street. There were miles and miles of bright-green rice fields flooded between dikes where carabao, or water buffalo, pulled wooden plows, and men and women in saggy knee pants and coolie hats worked in mucky gray mud from dawn till dusk.

Anna, our house girl, was in every way like an older sister to us. We would ride the streetcar with her to the *mauka* (mountain side) beginning of the Kalakaua beach road, where we'd get off and walk to the rice fields. We'd see women with large baskets of rice shoots bending over in the murky water, hand planting the rice. They wore protective bandanna scarves beneath their large coolie hats, and rolled the sleeves of their long, loose blouses up to their elbows.

At harvest time they joined the men in cutting the high, ripe grasses full of seed, which they shook vigorously on to the miller, and piled the chaff high into bundles of hay for sale and for their beasts. The rice was bagged in burlap sacks ready for loading on donkey carts to take to the market place.

Plowing a rice field with water buffalo, 1920. R. J. Baker, Bishop Museum

I walked the dikes with Anna and felt the soft, squishy mud and grass between my toes. It was always windy, so I had my brimmed hat tied under my chin. The trip to her grandma's was like an adventure to the Wizard of Oz. As we neared the house, I could already smell the tea brewing and the ginger marinade with soy sauce for the choice pieces of tender meat the old woman cooked on her open grate.

The house had a slanting tin roof and the door was always open for us to walk in and greet Anna's grandma. Her name was Popo, Chinese for grandma. She would stand beside one of her polished carved teak chairs, with thin silk brocaded cushions of bright blue or gold. She made her special oolong tea from Formosa, and served the piquant beverage in colorful hand-painted teacups with no handles. In the cup designs were flowers and symbols of good luck.

There were high chests with shiny brass handles and special long Chinese key locks. I know, because Popo would let me thread them through her special sealed cabinets like a magic wand to open them. On top of the chests sat faded sepia family photographs showing men in frog buttonhole shirts standing sedately with their stern-looking women seated before them—generations of Cantonese folk left behind in the ancient China homeland.

I had learned to ask Popo, "How are you?" in her native Cantonese—"Chow san, Popo?" And the tiny, frail lady in the black silk pajamas with pitifully bound knobby feet encased in black embroidered silk slippers would smile at me and pat my head. Her hair was long and shiny black, but sparse and drawn tightly up from her forehead into a neat bun, held in place with a long gold pin of 24-karat gold. All her jewelry was set in the soft, bright-yellow Chinese gold—the long, dangling earrings of dark, rich jade and diamonds that pulled her ear lobes out of shape; the heavy rings on her thin-veined fingers, the heart-shaped locket of jade and blood-red rubies around her scrawny neck, and the several circles of green, pink, and white jade bracelets on her tiny, age-spotted, emaciated arms.

Popo was the matriarch of those Pawa'a rice fields and she walked sedately in her station, wobbling on her broken little stilted feet. Her black eyes were keen and piercing and looked right through you. She spoke in her singsong, suck-in Cantonese dialect with her teenage granddaughter, of whom she was very proud. Anna was about to graduate from the eighth grade; an education was unknown to Chinese women in Popo's village.

The old woman always hobbled over to me and asked me to sit before her in a small replica of her throne chair, and she patted my little head again and smiled as she offered me a large, round, crisp almond wedding cookie or some candied kumquats, nuts, melon, squash, carrots, coconuts, or lychee she'd bought especially for us in A'ala Chinatown. Sometimes she'd give me a little bag of pine nuts to take home, along with some fortune cookies.

She always kept her tiny house neat and I was always afraid I'd put down the candy or cookie dishes on the wrong table, because each table featured a decoration: usually a special dish of fruit artistically arranged—big yellow pomelos, miniature mandarin oranges—or some punk and joss sticks burning in a dish filled with sand. There was her cooking wok and charcoal brazier with its smoky residue smell that haunted me long after we got home.

Beyond her hut stood the outhouse and a tin bathtub, with its water heated from a charcoal-lined pit beneath. Everywhere you looked were stacks of charcoal ready for lighting and cooking her dinner of freshly picked vegetables from the small garden around her house. She grew tender Chinese peas and string beans on bamboo stakes, green onions and chives, *won bok*, bamboo stalks with new edible shoots, beets, radishes, and watery beds of bean sprouts and water chestnuts.

Later I regretted having never learned Chinese or Japanese from the daily language schools my Oriental classmates attended after our regular school. The language schools flourished until America's distrust of all Orientals in World War II, when they were closed.

Years later, after I'd become a journalist, I had to get a story when Popo's rice growers were evicted from their fields to make way for low-cost Hawaiian housing. The Chinese farmers were irate and refused to leave. Accompanied by only a Chinese-speaking photographer, I approached an elderly man who wore a coolie hat and held a huge pitchfork in his hand. When he learned we were from the press, he lunged at us with his pitchfork and we literally had to run for our lives! The astute photographer got a shot of me being chased by the man with the sharp spikes of his implement only inches from my face!

Trips We Took

Gearing up the old Model T Ford for a day's outing took a week's preparation, including washing out the Thermos bottle with baking soda for potable water, which wasn't available at spots like Lanikai on the Windward side, or Hanauma Bay.

The Pali Road in those days was a two-lane dirt highway cut through the pass that natives had used for centuries. In my folks' time, horses and buggies often got swept over the misty cliffs when it was windy. Later when we rode over the Pali in the old Ford with no seat belts, on rainy days we skidded on the almost impassable muddy road. Often we'd come to some nearly upside-down halt, wedged in the gullies alongside the gooey lanes, where we waited for passersby to help get our spinning wheels out with levered boards and everybody pushing. There was always a drink of cold, fresh, spring-fed water at the hairpin turn, or rest at the Half Way House along the way to Kailua.

Bordering the Pali Road stood low wooden railings painted white for visibility, but they were scant reassurance against the threat of cars careening over the precipitous side. We clutched one another and sucked on sugar cane on our way to visit friends with a beach home in Lanikai. By the time we got to the last bridge from Kailua, we had sucked the stalks dry and spat out the pulp, and had the flaky sugar cane fibers stuck between our wiggly baby teeth.

The very last bridge on our journey spanned Ka'elepulu Stream. It was a rickety, feeble thing of decaying planks, and we had to get out and walk across to make the car lighter to maneuver. We walked the hot sandy trails from the rolling sand dunes into the new 1923 subdivision that was incorrectly named "Lanikai" by *haole* realtors (it should have been called "Kailani" in correct Hawaiian, or "Ko'olaupoko").

Japanese farmers with large straw hats and neck scarves, long-sleeved shirts and gloves, tended sprawling vines of watermelons, (a dollar for two) and sweet cantaloupes that they often cut open for you to sample on the spot. One taste and you had to buy a whole sweet melon to quench your thirst.

I remember the strong wind blowing as we ran on the Ka 'Iwa ridge trail overlooking the bay with the Mokulua Islands, tops of old craters, and a few fishing shacks on the hot barren land. It wasn't until the thirties that folks planted trees—coco palms and monkeypod and Norfolk pines—to fringe the famous shoreline, formerly reserved for royalty. Kailua had the largest coconut grove on the island, planted by *ali'i*.

Finely pumiced coral of the white sandy beaches of Lanikai were graced with vines of sky-blue beach morning glories, and yellow and salmon-red beach sweet peas against clumps of sturdy *naupaka*, with its legendary half-flowers of white and ball seed pods like Kaua'i's *mokihana*. Also covering the rolling sand dunes were tufts of prickly *'aki'aki* grass that protected the beach from eroding in heavy winter storms and high tides. Across from the beach road were fields of gaillardias and groves of ironwood trees brought in from Australia for windbreaks.

A huge lava-rock fish god altar guarded the entrance to the bay—an arresting stone platform with an upright phallic symbol where King Kamehameha himself worshipped and watched shadows of fish in the aqua water below. Seabirds, harbingers of a good catch, signaled where to lay the *hukilau* nets for the lu'au feasts to come.

Today the Mokuluas are bird sanctuaries where shearwaters nest in sandy burrows, and migrating *kolea*, or golden plover, sleep at night after their spectacular 6,000-mile nonstop flight here from their Arctic homes during winter. Today they are banded for study of flight and breeding patterns. Soon, alas, there will be no more secrets of nature to disclose!

If we decided to travel north, we'd stop for guava picking along the way or picnic near Sacred Falls and leave beneath the smooth stream rocks our leaf offering to the pig god Kamapua'a. Fuchsia blossoms of the mountain apple trees fell to make rich magenta carpeting on the forest floor, where *menehune* hid in blue-eyed *honohono* grass, we really believed.

A quick swim in the icy cold stream, washing our hair with red shampoo ginger, and squishing red mud from between bare toes quickened the appetite for peanut butter and banana sandwiches and lemonade.

We'd stop for shelling along the shore by the old Boys Reform School at Waiale'e and find whole cowries, cone shells, and dried starfish and sea urchins for our special displays at home or to take to school.

At the Kahuku Sugar Mill we'd fill jars with warm crystals of raw sugar to take home for our oatmeal porridge, scooping up handfuls for tasting right then. The aroma of sugar cane boiling into brown sugar is one of lasting favorite smells from my childhood. We'd often stop along the road to cut stalks of ripe sugar cane, which we'd peel and cut off into small lengths to bite into and suck on. Now they use those leftovers to make canec for buildings.

Before Waimea Bay, we'd stop again to explore tide pools and catch long-tailed, slithery black fish and limpets in tide pools. We hiked up Waimea Valley on a single muddy trail to swim under the falls. There was no fee, no park, no planted gardens, just the natural rain forest of old Hawai'i. Occasionally we would see fierce, black wild boar rooting in the bushes, scaring us with their loud snorts and grunts. The big ones hunters pursued in the dry valleys in Wai'anae, Niu, and Kuli'ou'ou.

We'd often spend weekends at Mokuleia Beach at a friend's house with a second-story loft view window. For hours we'd sit up there and watch porpoises leap in the surf. We bought papayas, bananas, mountain apples, mangoes, and poi at stands along the winding Kamehameha Highway, once the King's Highway. The taste of all those fruits and vegetables was different then, perhaps because it was never put on scales to be weighed, but just cost "two for a quatta" or "5 cen' one."

Going to Hanauma Bay for a supper picnic was quite an outing, as the road ended where Hawai'i Kai high-rises begin today. On the ride to Hanauma, Dad would check out the car at Wailupe, and we kids would run up the cliff to a secret Hawaiian burial cave we had found. What excitement to see a canoe with bones carefully wrapped in tree fern *pulu*, and nearby the adzes, koa bowls, treasured hair *lei palaoa* with pendants of whale bone, and gourds! We didn't dare remove anything, as graves like these were sacred to the gods, our Hawaiian friends told us.

We parked the old "tin Lizzy" and loaded up our gear of hibachi, blankets, salad, and homemade cornbread, and hiked the rest of the way over the lava of Koko Head promontory, winding our way down to the beach through precarious footholds on sharp outcroppings.

Our feet were so tough we could walk on the rough coral along the steep slopes to Hanauma Bay before the road was made in 1937. We would explore the many tide pools at Hanauma and catch slippery black snake fish or hermit crabs with our hands and then let them go free. Or we'd find slime-covered cowrie shells in sea lettuce with our toes along the edges of the tide pools. Today the shells are gone and the few left on the near reefs of Wai'anae are protected by law from shell collectors.

We had a fish fry over the open fire of *kiawe* driftwood with succulent fresh mullet, or *ulua*, just caught in the circular throw nets of the Hawaiian fishermen on the beach, who usually joined us in our feast.

Visiting friends at 'Ewa plantation was also a safari for picking tiny wild tomatoes and *poha* along the two-lane dirt road that kicked up a lot of dust as we later drove by in our new open ranch automobile with its collapsible top, always too heavy to attach before the rain soaked us.

We watched spectacular horse shows at Schofield Barracks, something like Hawaiian Ascot races where all the ladies donned their best Gibson Girl finery, with high-buttoned shoes, elbow-length gloves, and wide horsehair hats tied on with chiffon scarves.

Sunday afternoon tea was like a fashion parade for the ladies at Moanalua Gardens, part of the Damon estate open to the public. Carp swam in the Oriental pools, and we kids wore matching outfits like our mothers' and ran over quaint bridges where a freeway ramp today leaps skyward as part of H-1 on the way to Honolulu International Airport.

I took my grandson with me to see the last vestige of the only Salt Lake in Hawai'i being dynamited to be filled in with concrete by developers for a golf course and condominiums. The day was eventful only because we found the first and oldest petrified wood in the bowels of the already drained lake.

Girl Scouts

Hiking on muddy trails to the cold waterfalls in Manoa and Waimea Valley or Sacred Falls as Girl Scouts, we learned firsthand about the rain forests just off the main roads. We learned the story of steep Sacred Falls and why we had to place a leaf beneath a stone as an offering to the pig god Kamapua'a. Some of the leaves were bare skeletons that had been put there long ago and were never removed in fear of Kamapua'a.

Once he was the fierce hog god who devastated the forests, and the warriors of a neighboring village were ordered to capture him and his people with him. He was cornered at the end of the Sacred Falls trail and the people were screaming for help.

Before his pursuers reached him, he miraculously heaved and puffed and his body became so swollen his head reached the top of the cliffs surrounding the falls. His bristles became spikes that served as a ladder for his people to climb up to reach safety before the enemy warriors arrived. As the last person reached safety, Kamapua'a shrunk to normal size and scurried up the trail unharmed. So, in deference to his help, he is forever remembered by those who walk the muddy trail up to Sacred Falls today.

When we hiked to the Pali from town, we walked on the tropical winding Old Pali Road, with waterfalls dashing down to the pool below where hikers filled their canteens with refreshing cold mountain water.

We wore denim "sailor *moku*" bell-bottom slacks (not called "jeans" yet), tailor-made for $2.50, and blue-and-white plaid *palaka* shirts, and *lauhala* hats we purchased at plantation stores, and white tennis shoes which we often discarded for bare feet.

Around our necks we wore red bandannas clasped with bolos we made (as part of Girl Scout crafts) out of dry *kukui* nuts that we gathered at the beach. We laboriously cut through the hard nuts with a tiny hand saw, and left a band across one side for the scarf to go through. We gouged out all the odoriferous *kukui* seeds and then sand-papered the nuts smooth, using the natural oil to give them a high polish of shiny jet black.

As we walked along the trails, we picked clusters of *palapalai* fern and woodland *pikake*, which we made into *haku* leis for our heads or hats. They smelled like the rain forest around us. If ginger were in bloom, we could also weave the fragrant yellow or white blossoms into the leis.

If it were really hot and humid, we would hunt for clumps of *awapuhi*—red shampoo ginger—which we would squeeze on top of our sweaty heads. The liquid was slickly mushy and felt like shampoo, which we could wash off in one of the many fresh-water pools in the forest.

When our camp opened up in Pearl City next to the harbor, we rode the famous O'ahu Railway and Land Co. train that we boarded at A'ala Park. The trip on the train made it seem like we were really going to some faraway place, and we sang songs and played our 'ukuleles and harmonicas.

The camp at Pearl City was full of long, squirmy, fat centipedes that wound themselves around our tent poles, got inside pillow slips and hiking shoes, and bred prolifically until the ugly buffo marianus toads were imported from the Philippines to eat them. Other centipedes were tiny, brilliant shiny green ones that also gave a potent sting, especially if you were allergic to the venom, as I was.

Another train trip went all the way up the North Shore to Mokule'ia before Camp Erdman was built. Here, we watched pods of humpback whales breaching and schools of playful porpoise. We could collect beautiful whole shells on the miles of pristine beach sand dunes, now an eyesore of discarded cars and other rubbish.

Another camp was in 'Ahuimanu Valley, where counselors used the original stone lava rock building of the first Catholic monastic training school for teachers as our camp headquarters. Nearby nestled a shady swimming hole carved out of the red clay soil.

At Maunawili we used the original ranch house of the Castle family for our Girl Scout spread, and we loaded into a farm truck to ride through sugar cane fields, or hiked to swim at a sparkling, cold spring pool fringed with delicate maiden-hair fern. We camped near trails crowded with sweet strawberry guavas.

Today the valley contains tract homes and horse stables, and the bathing pool has been filled in and its spring diverted for irrigation.

I learned to smoke at a Maui Girl Scout camp as a counselor! A nurse gave me my first pack of medicated Cubebs to stop my hay fever from all the ginger around, and it helped dry up my bloodied nose.

Our camp was called "Papa Baldwin's," as he had given us pristine land behind Ha'iku on the road to Hana. We had idyllic waterfalls and crystal clear freshwater pools when I took my Brownies and went skinny-dipping and got reprimanded for it!

Today the camp and its waterfall and the surrounding crystal pools are no more, as they were covered by a severe earthquake; but the jungle has covered the area with new ferns and flowers as though no time has passed.

Sea Creatures

From the time I can remember, we explored tide pools at Kahala or Hanauma Bay, watching miniature *manini* (black and white striped prisoner fish), velvety long-tailed black fish, hermit crabs, sea urchins, cowries in green lettuce seaweed, yellow tangs and wrasses, parrot fish and Moorish idol, *kihikihi*.

I would watch as the funny mole crabs would suddenly appear out of nowhere at the shorebreak and grab the long nettled tails of the Portuguese-man-of-war and pull them down into the bubbling sand. These crabs run backwards and look like ancient horseshoe crabs with plates on their backs.

The man-of-war jellyfish bubbles looked like sails of Portuguese sailing ships and so got their name. My mate used to say he knew they were men-of-war because I got stung on the bosom! And once when I went to the clinic for treatment after a bad sting, the smiling doc recorded my injury as a "Person-of-War" lesion!

As toddlers, when we'd walk the beach we'd see shellfish clinging to rocks in low tide, and my dad always taught us the names of the tiny creatures: limpets, one-valve shellfish with ribbed stone coolie hats; turban and cone *opihi*, often eaten raw by the fishermen.

Once I swam in 100 yards from a raft at Hale'iwa with a baby octopus curled around my arm. I guess he liked me.

We'd catch large ghost crabs at night by shining our flashlights on them and they'd scamper into buried tin cans with bait tied on a string across. Then we'd let them all go. They have intricate corkscrew burrows; and when they have piles of large sand mounds on the beach, they are looking for mates and we call this our sexy beach.

Sometimes we'd see schools of fish so thick and black they'd look like coral, only they'd move. When we walked into them at low tide we could see a milling mass of tiny silver *'oama*, which are the juvenile *weke*.

Eels would slither out of coral *puka* (holes) and take meat out of my hand. I had a pet leopard eel that would ward me off if I got too close, and I respected him. Sometimes we'd find a pure white eel on the beach, along with hammerhead or reef sharks netted by fishermen and left to float to shore and die.

We learned never to bother the green sea turtles that surfed in our bays before they became endangered by too many people hunting them. The turtle shells became trophies and their flesh ended up as turtle steaks or in soup.

Probably the most fascinating of all the sea creatures I loved as a girl were the nudibranchs or sea slugs, especially the bright orange and red Spanish dancers, which would pretend to die and sink to the ocean bed. But, if you lifted up the slippery things and put them in a glass jar, you could watch the magnificent undulating dance that gave them their name.

They have two eyes, fringed with long lashes on their flat heads, and delicate twirling ruching, like revolving lace scalloped around their restless bodies: a joy to children on the beach. Today I catch them for visiting kids to watch. They usually live far out on the reef and, when they float to shore with the currents, they usually die on the sand.

Flying fish are another favorite for children to watch, along with graceful stingrays that hide beneath the sand, often exposing only their lethal, sharp spiny tails. At night we would dig up bits of phosphorescence from the wet beach to carry along as glowing magic.

The sea has its mysteries, like why thousands of puffer fish float up dead on the beach, or occasionally *chloeia flava*, rare orange-red sea caterpillars with numerous delicate white feet. They are related to stinging fire worms but do no harm and come from depths as far as 2,000 feet below.

Strolling the beach, we got to know the seabirds as our friends—like the wandering tattler or *'ulili*, named for its cry. It is usually alone, poking its long beak into the sand to search for food; sleek white boobies, with red feet that look like hot-water bottles; shearwaters that nest offshore on islets and moan like ghosts haunting a house; gliding *'iwa*, or frigate birds, with a 7-foot wing span, the widest of any bird for the size of its body (its Hawaiian name means "robber," because it steals fish from other birds in flight).

The pure-white fairy tern that hovers in flight like an osprey will come to you if you clap your hands. It lays a single egg delicately balanced on a bare branch and can be seen today at Kapi'olani Park, returning with fish for its young.

Today at our home in Lanikai we watch humpback whales cavorting as they breach high in the water, splashing down their immense bodies to make whirlpools of foam visible for miles around.

Schools of porpoises were familiar to us offshore when we stayed at Kawela Bay or Mokule'ia, and we pretended they were our pet whales.

In all my life I have never lived where I could not see, smell, or hear the sea, a part of my being. I believe I once was a tiny electric blue fish, the kind I saw in Tahiti; and when I leave this planet, I will join a school of blue fish, sort of "coming home."

My Beach Today

Today, only an hour's drive from the city, I sit in a cove silent of man-made sounds and listen to the waves lapping on the shore...a soothing, slushing sound with an almost monotonous obligato...never jarring, never discordant, always pleasant to listen to.

Beyond—a mile out—is the hushed crescendo of the surf breaking on the reef...like the muted rhythm of a faraway sea train with a surging beat that does not annoy, a kind of pianissimo thundering far, far away, like the bass in a symphony orchestra blending in with the more tender treble strings.

I lie in a vacuum of restfulness on my beach in the caressing sunshine and feel the warmth penetrate my very bones. From beneath my sunhat over my face I watch the quiet life around me, have time to count the rollings back and forth of the pieces of sandstone, coral, and black lava rock as they turn and return up near the scalloped end of the wave to break on shore and then are rolled all the way back again seaward; a lesson in philosophy...the ups and downs and the never-knowing-exactly-where of life.

Tiny sand crabs scamper against the white sand, skittering sideways, always furtive, their tubular eyes up like colorless gelatine jujubes. They seem to hear even my heartbeat, they are so sensitive to sound. I hold my breath and they come toward my beach mat. If I lift my head up, they vanish, running in staccato beat to their holes, entering sidesaddle, with a special alert before disappearing.

I read a doctor's dissertation on these ghost crabs...how their dens go down deep, clockwise in myriads of spiral whirls.

The leaves of the nearby *hau* tree fall silently like tiny sails in a gentle breeze, a fluttering dance to the tune of the sea breeze.

The delight to watch very near shore is the Spanish dancer or nudibranch, a gorgeous orange-red sea slug like a baby ray, with furled ruching or tiny ruffles along its delicate, sinuous body. It's only about six inches long, but tantalizes as it coquettishly flirts with its voluptuous wings literally afire, as the sunlight catches the golds and crimsons of its tiny being. Its oversized eyes protrude from the flat top of its head like someone had pasted unmatching buttons on a sewing pattern.

Another joy is to wade along the shoreline and stand still in knee-deep water, as schools of silvery fish swim in and out between your legs, darting swiftly in one direction, then changing quickly in another as they follow their leader.

And still another joy is to snorkel just a few yards offshore over a coral head and watch all kinds of sea life perform. I have a pet moray eel that comes out when I approach her rocks. She's leopard-spotted in chartreuse and black. I respect her territory and swim away if she says I'm too close.

The fish beneath me in just over a few feet of water are beautiful...combinations only an artist can produce. I like their forms better than their scientific names that I can never remember and don't do them justice anyhow, so I name them myself...Golden Gilda, leopard sea snake, pink shocker. There's the brilliant-yellow butterflyfish, the goatfish, the squirrelfish, the tiger-striped one edged in gold leaf, the shocking pink striped candy cane one, the tiny iridescent blue one, the bloated porcupinefish.

Every once in awhile we see a trio of giant manta rays close offshore, flaunting themselves like macabre dancers in flawless rhythm.

Another of the delicate creatures is the floating violet sea snail, the size of a quarter, that floats upside down with a colorless jellybean-like foot that brings it across miles of sea to shore. It is classified as rare in Hawai'i's shell book. The brilliant-purple dye inside that settles in the bottom of its delicate orchid-tinted shell was used for royalty in the days of Cleopatra.

At night there is mysterious phosphorescence glowing in the wet sand with its bluish "angel light of the heavens."

The true giants of the sea viewed from our dining table are humpback whales come here again for winter calving. We watch while they breach and displace tons of water as they thrash their monstrous tails high in the air and crash into the choppy sea, then spout as if to signal that we mustn't forget that they, too, exist in my ocean.

The Fish Market

What excitement it was to go along with Dad when he inspected the A'ala fish market in Chinatown early on Saturday mornings!

From blocks away the rich, primitive, unmistakable aroma of fish would greet us and pull us in, past the two-story tenement buildings with corrugated tin roofs along River Street. As we walked through the pre-dawn darkness, there were competing smells of Chinese food cooking on woks, of tamarind trees and of the river itself. But the fish and Daddy's large hands drew us along inexorably. The fish auction was held before sunrise, and we watched as the huge 10-foot marlin and yellowfin tuna were unloaded from trucks and horse-and-buggy carts with Chinese, Japanese, and Hawaiian fishermen vying for special places along the wide, slippery floor to best display their catch ready for the auction.

I shall always remember the vivid display of tropical fish for sale. The colors were reminiscent of a huge rainbow dismembered into sparkling phosphorescence on the wet floor that also reflected the colors again. The colors of the fish themselves were enough to enjoy at the fish auction. Blue, green, or scarlet parrot fish, silver *ulua*, and baby *papio*, shiny mullet, red and blue snappers (mother's favorites for baking whole in ti leaves), and myriads of smaller tangs and wrasse.

Out of buckets, octopus were still climbing with their sucking tentacles moving them on top of moray and white eels with vicious-looking teeth; alongside were Samoan and rock sea crabs, clawless spiny and slippery lobsters akin to crayfish, and baskets of all kinds of *opihi* or shellfish and fragrant, succulent *limu* or seaweed.

As the auction began, the buyers' voices rose higher and higher in an Oriental Babylon—Chinese, Japanese, and Hawaiian in a harmonious pidgin everyone understood.

Across the way, the Chinese and Hawaiians were readying their neat stalls, divided by glass partitions. Customers lined up with their string shopping bags ready to be filled. The fishmongers' fresh white aprons were not yet bloodied, as they began to display their rainbow harvest of the sea in artistic fashion, usually by color. The vendors hung up the limp octopus and eels, and arranged the small fish to overlap one another on the display counters like ripples on the waves. Sometimes the still viable octopus would make one last try for freedom and squirt black ink at us outside the glass enclosures.

Already the crowds were pushing and shouting as they bargained back and forth for the right price before making a firm purchase. The fishmongers wrapped the fish or crabs in thick white butcher paper and added bunches of fresh *limu*, or seaweed, with the briny smell of the sea, or handfuls of live shellfish.

When we left the market, we'd head for our favorite fruit and vegetable stalls, which also included candy chews, jars of Oriental seeds and plums, and boxes of dried lychee nuts. We always got gifts of candy or fruit of our choice from the head man with gold teeth who smiled as he patted our heads— bright red-dyed coconut balls, crackseed, caramels, crisp puffed rice squares with peanuts or gooey, chewy ones with sesame seeds; and for mother, who disliked all our crackseed favorites, a box of wrinkled but sweet dried lychees or puffed rice candy squares.

After the market Dad would take us into a narrow Chinese restaurant for breakfast of egg roll, noodles, *chow mein*, *dim sum* (dumplings with sweet beans or chopped pork and vegetables inside), crisp *gau gee* (with more meat) and, of course, weak tea served in round cups with no handles but painted with pretty birds or butterflies.

As we left, we usually got candy favors from "the boss," the Chinese man in charge who knew Dad and had little treats ready for us to pick up. We hated to leave our beloved place in Chinatown.

After the market Dad always let us walk leisurely along bustling Chinatown's King Street, which continued leeward as the main road to the heights of Wahiawa or 'Ewa and Wai'anae, all two-lane dirt roads through waving green fields of sugar cane.

Going uptown we visited the many Chinese stores selling yardage from the Orient. You could buy heavy pongee suiting for 75 cents a yard, raw silk for two bits, and silk brocade for 50 cents! I usually made all my own clothes, even tailored suits for college, choosing from an array of bolts directly from

Hong Kong or Shanghai.

You could choose hand-embroidered Chinese slippers to match the pajamas you made and buy frog fasteners to match. In the thirties it was the vogue for wide-bottomed beach pajamas fashioned out of cretonne curtain material with large floral designs. We also wore fitted wrap-around split skirts to match our new boyish bobs, closely shingled coiffures now in vogue again.

Our open-toed shoes were fastened with grosgrain ribbon bows and painted in wild colors with many coats of thick, quick-drying lacquer, like nail polish.

We all had our individual ornately carved, black teak hope chests inlaid with mother-of-pearl. Mine, however, was filled with books of poetry and novels instead of exquisitely hand-embroidered linens. There were guest towels, dresser scarves, tablecloths and matching napkins, and cloisonné trays, jewelry boxes, and carved ivory, now tabu in our country.

There were miniature salt and nut dishes and complete sets of delicate translucent Canton china with China markings on the bottom of the teacups or round and square plates. Today it is all ersatz, made in Japan and merely hand decorated in Hong Kong or Taiwan. And marked to say so. But then everything was real, and no markings needed to exclaim the fact. It was as unmistakable and true and beautiful as the smell of fresh fish on market day.

Boat Day

Boat Day began in Hawai'i in the mid-1870s, when the Pacific Mail Steamship Company brought precious monthly mail from "the continent."

In 1883, sugar king Claus Spreckels made a record run from San Francisco to Hawai'i on his ship, the first *Mariposa*, in 15 days, 21 hours. Capt. William Matson brought his bride to Hawai'i on the brigantine *Lurline* in 1887, in 14 days from the Bay City; and then in 1901 he founded the Matson Navigation Company, which owned the beach hotels and brought mainland visitors in hordes to Waikiki. (Today the hotels are owned by the Japanese.)

A second *Lurline* was running in 1908, the *Wilhelmina* and *Sierra* in 1910, the *Matsonia* in 1912-13 with World War I service, and the *Manoa* and *Maui* in 1917. The first luxury ship was the *Malolo* in the early 1930s, followed by the *Mariposa* and *Monterey* in 1932 and the third *Lurline* in 1933. The *Malolo* became the luxury *Matsonia* in 1938.

"Boat Day," as such, was in its Victorian heyday in 1907, with Capt. Henry Berger's Royal Hawaiian band in full swing at the pier at the foot of Richards Street. Gibson girls in wasp-waisted gowns, garden hats, parasols, and high-buttoned shoes were throwing and catching serpentine streamers. Straw-hatted men did the same, and they all watched the eager diving boys alongside the docks.

On Boat Day, island boys serenaded locals and guests on the moonlit lawns beneath the shade trees as we sang along, and anyone who wished danced the hula on call to the sounds of 'ukulele and string and steel guitars.

Aloha Tower appeared in 1925 to dominate Honolulu Harbor—184 feet high, with 10 stories, a water tank for offices below, and a light visible for 20 miles at sea.

The Matsonia Steamer landing in 1924 on "Boat Day." R. J. Baker, Bishop Museum

Model T Fords filled stalls in the newly planted Irwin Park at the foot of Bishop Street. There were ships from all over the world traveling all over the world. Island stopovers were festive affairs for visitors as well as islanders. There were no plane flights between Hawai'i and the mainland until 1936, and then it took 20 hours for 4-engine propeller "flying boats" to make the trip that cost $278 one way or $500 round trip.

Passengers could have a luxury 5-day cruise on board a Matson liner for only $85 cabin fare; teachers, government employees, and students, $65. Beef tea was served on deck chair-side at mid-morning, high tea in the afternoon, and a gourmet dinner of several entrées and scrumptious desserts. There were shuffleboard and "horse races" on deck, card games in the elaborate mirrored lounge, and dancing in the salon every night till dawn to the tune of live orchestras. Lounges held revolving chairs and a Steinway piano. And for readers there was an ample library.

In this milieu, Boat Day evolved as one of the highlights of island life in the pre-air travel days of Hawai'i in the thirties. One began preparing for Boat Day a week before it happened. Folks eagerly scanned the passenger lists in the newspaper, noting celebrities—movie stars and concert musicians, turbaned sheiks, presidents, princes, and their retinues, and kings—en route to the Orient or Australia on world tours. In the thirties and forties, the beach hotels and off-port ship interviews were my beat as a journalist for the local press.

On Boat Day you met friends at the old Alexander Young Hotel lobby or coffee shop (demolished in the seventies for the new high-rise Pauahi Towers and Tamarind Park) or around the counter on Fort and Hotel Streets at Benson Smith's drugstore, the equivalent of an English pub in those days. The big parade surged down Bishop and Fort Streets, mushrooming as executives and secretaries from nearby offices closed shop to join the pulsating throng to meet the steamship liner, whose arrival was the big event of the week in old Honolulu town. The air was heavy with the mixed scents of flower leis, the excited crowd getting bigger and the leis heavier on the arms of the marching mass of excited people.

We had no traffic lights then. Sweating Hawaiian traffic cops in starched khaki uniforms with white pith helmets stood in the middle of cross streets on platforms beneath tan umbrellas directing carts, cars, and pedestrians with graceful movements of their white-gloved hands. When there was a lull in the traffic, the cops climbed down and danced the hula to the delight of the crowd! The police officers also had a famous Glee Club, and won awards for their singing and playing guitars and 'ukuleles as the "Singing Cops of Hawai'i!"

There was an ambience of Mardi Gras, a tingling excitement in the air as movie stars, kids home from college, visitors, and family arrived. There were no designated lei stands, just streetside lei sellers, male and female, holding up cascading garlands of tropical flowers. The bronze faces of the sellers, often toothless, were etched in lines of smiles and contentment. Plump Hawaiian women sitting on the curbside strung lei after lei, and there was an overwhelming aroma of yellow plumeria or *melia* (then called graveyard flowers), tuberose, gardenias, carnations—heady mixed perfumes. Boas of shiny green *maile*, fresh from the mountains of the Big Island, were entwined with bright-orange crepe paper leis to resemble real *'ilima*, O'ahu's island flower.

Most leis were "two for a quatta" except for the thicker carnation wreaths, which went for 50 cents and 75 cents. *Maunaloa* leis, the tropical sweet pea vine strung in buds with petals turned down like scales on a lavender snake, were also 50 cents. There were no small vanda orchid leis, as the florists had not yet imported the plants from the Philippines.

There were *haku* or flat headbands, also worn on hats, woven with delicate fishtail or *laua'e* fern with dainty baby roses, corn flowers or bachelor buttons entwined.

Lei sellers wore *holomu'u* or shorter mu'umu'us and *lauhala* hats with *haku* leis as bands. The sellers smiled at customers and called many by their first names. "You goin' meet your sweethaht? I geeve you one extra flowa, one beeg gardeenya, yeah? Bumbye you smell good, no?"

There was the sound of clippety, scurrying, shuffling feet in shoes and *geta*, Japanese wooden slippers, along the rough sidewalk and up the old termite-ridden wooden stairs of Pier 9—thumping and pounding, shoving ahead to get a good place along the railing to see friends as the ship finally reached the dock. Hundreds of hot, sweaty bodies of excited people on the second floor of the pier squirming in position to say aloha. Everybody was meeting somebody—like a huge reunion of the whole town—relatives, friends, businessmen, old teachers, classmates.

Armfuls of flower leis clung to dripping wet bodies in the moist humid heat. Hats awry were crushed and bent out of shape as folks continued to push through the steadily growing crowd, now being held back by barriers around the Royal Hawaiian Band, which blared with brass and woodwinds and steel guitars the nostalgic songs everyone knew—"'Akaka Falls" with the tremulous falsetto voice of Lena Machado, "Hawai'i's songbird," reaching to the rooftops of the rusted, weathered corrugated ceiling and beyond; "The Song of the Islands," that left you "chicken-skinned" and teary-eyed, as the white steamship heaved and creaked against the rubber tires cushioning the pilings of the dock below. Hawaiian stevedores shouted out mooring directions in guttural Hawaiian and pidgin while they caught the thick rope tow lines. Finally the swinging, banging gangway was attached to the liner.

All eyes strained. The ship's bow quietly cleared the corner of the pier and sloshed alongside the wharf. Tears unashamedly misted many eyes. Eager voices cried out for friends and relatives aboard. An electrifying tremor passed through the crowd when the band finally surged into the martial strains of "Hawai'i Pono'i," our anthem, followed by a lively hula with everyone swaying and clapping in rhythmic beat. Cries vied with music; frenetic bodies moved in a sweltering mass, inching nearer the railing of the pier to wave and shout to special passengers aboard.

Bells clanged, whistles blared, passengers stood shoulder to shoulder in hot steamy passageways waiting to descend down the gangway to Paradise. Off they came, waving and shouting to the crowds below who greeted their loved ones with embraces and leis.

The meeting was a chaotic mass of tears and joy, leis piled high with crushed petals falling in a shower of confetti beneath bare feet, slippers, and squeaky new mainland pumps and oxfords.

Suitcases were gathered up with steamer rugs, and babies thrust into *kupuna* arms. Serpentine lines of people zig-zagged away from the docks—men and women arm-in-arm, squeezing, kissing, hugging, and laughing, cheeks smudged with lipstick. Long lines of cars around Irwin Park filled with happy faces of lei-bedecked passengers. Islanders were eager to show their visitors around or take them for a refreshing swim before lunch.

As the crowds dispersed, the bargains began with unsold leis going for half-price or less, more given away free with a purchase. This was the time bosses sent their girl Fridays out to pick up leis for dates that night. Diving boys scooped up soggy leis from the water to wear around their heads or necks for fun.

Later other parents hurried by with steamer trunks and footlockers ready for the next sailing out when their kids would depart for college. There was a smell of mothballs from borrowed sweaters and coats, gloves and leotards for the freezing weather on the east coast. Always tucked beneath clothes and books was a cache of crackseed and lychees, glazed pineapple and candied coconut, squash, melon rind, and ginger, and *lauhala* placemats and shell leis for main-land gifts.

Young college departees came to the ship in their new fall mainland outfits, sweltering in the latest woolen knit sweaters and skirts, long silk stockings attached to garter belts (no panty hose yet), and carrying gloves to show they knew how to dress for sorority rushes at Wellesley, Smith, or Vassar.

The guys wore athletic pullovers with dad's football letters and baggy pleated trousers and new felt hats with ear-muffs turned up! If you could afford to go to a costly mainland name college, you bought a wardrobe to prove it or carried a borrowed raccoon or camel's hair topcoat on your arm in proud drudgery!

Everyone you ever knew boarded the ship to say aloha and have a sequestered nip of booze in your cramped state-room or a soft drink at the Prohibition bar in the lounge. Piled-up leis covered your ears, and almost your nose, and you carried the rest on both arms as you waddled around on deck feverishly clutching last-minute directives from the family to visit relatives and write home.

Finally the milling crowd shuffled off in a hesitant single file down the creaking gangway, folks looking back for a last wave, blowing kisses. Passengers lined up every inch of the ship's dockside railing and their colored serpentine streamers made sagging fluttering rainbows in the hot noonday sun. Moist fingers tugged at the last curls of the paper ribbons across the harbor as the band played the poignant strains of "Aloha Oe." It was now the real departure, the leaving of home as an adult for a lifetime, the breaking away as the tangled masses of multicolored paper streamers broke and tore free in a glorious confusion of aloha. Half-choked cries drifted in between the wails of music and clanking chains as the ship pulled out. "Don't forget to write... and see Aunt Emma..." Handkerchiefs and scarves waved and waved as the bow of the liner stubbornly turned, pushed by heaving pilot tugboats to head northeast to California.

The crowds ran down to cars and drove to Pier 2, where they continued to wave and shout aloha until the ship became a blurred smear of color above a gleaming white hull, and it steamed out past the vast blue Pacific horizon.

There was a painful letdown as you slowly strolled back to your car and silently got in, wearing the lei you had caught from shipside. You breathed a kiss on it as you lowered your head in the deep fragrance of another aloha.

Diving Boys

Hawai'i's diving boys in the twenties and thirties considered their occupation an art and took great pride in belonging to one of the few traditional groups of the Islands. They are now only a historical legend.

Thousands of passengers on the busy liners entering or leaving Honolulu harbor were intrigued, watching the angular brown-skinned lads as they plunged into the green waters alongside the ship. The boys laughed and shouted in their own pidgin vernacular, enticing wide-eyed *malihini* to pitch them shiny coins. The Scottish comedian, Harry Lauder, tied his on a string which he'd pull up and use over and over again, 'tis said. The boys had eager expressions on their faces, with flashing white teeth and irritated, red, salt-burned eyes, and they smiled teasingly at those aboard while they splashed their lithe bodies about like porpoises playing at sea.

Sometimes they collected only nickels from cheapskates, but didn't have time to check as they would slip the coins into cheek-caches in their parched mouths. Their careers were not profitable when only troop ships arrived during World War II, and they managed to average barely $2 a ship apiece, sometimes less, for their hour's swim in the greasy waters at the docks. Two dollars an hour was not a bad rate then but, unfortunately for the boys, the ships didn't come in or depart 8 hours a day.

A diver had to show real skill before he was permitted to engage in this dangerous and thrilling occupation. The boys were organized under the Hawaiian Divers Association (which during its heyday was composed of 21 senior and 17 junior members) for the purpose of setting up rules of safety and conduct for its divers. It was no cinch dodging the swirling propellers of the huge passenger liners. In pre-war days two boys were drowned in the whirlpool suction created by the backwash of the propellers.

When a boy was ready to join the group, he had to prove his aquatic abilities and be able to dive 12 feet or more after

Diving boys on a barge, 1920–30. Bishop Museum

a shiny coin, grasp it in his hand and return to the surface waving the money for the donor to see before stuffing it into his mouth which bulged with coins after a morning's workout.

As a test, novices were taken to the docks and required to dive into current-filled waters as a ship actually pulled out of the harbor, then swim 200 yards. Senior members, 17 years and up, were given the whole area of the ship as their territory in which to dive for coins, but for juniors from 13 to 16, only the middle and front parts of the ship were allowed, for their own safety.

The boys were registered with the Police Department's Crime Prevention Bureau for protection and had to follow specific police directives. They had to dress at the "three nail open corner" at Pier 7 before diving over the seawall into the harbor to Pier 9, where the big liners arrived and departed. They had to leave the docks there immediately after the ship sailed, and return to Pier 7.

In the thirties, the boys had a make-shift boat shack on the shore at Ala Moana and actually lived on the money they caught diving at shipside. A tin "kitty" held all the coins collected, and the boys bought food with their meager earnings. They washed their few clothes in the ocean and prepared their meals from scanty canned goods they purchased along with poi, and they managed to survive in a very modest manner.

In the forties the boathouse was gone and with it the ability for the diving boys to make ends meet with shipside earnings alone, so they also took other jobs. George Hanawahine, at 33 a strong, well-built Hawaiian, came all the way from his home in Waimanalo to dive for money. He and his brothers, Joseph and Abel, fished with their circular throw net offshore from home and sold fish at the A'ala Park auction to make a go of it. Other boys did housework, yardwork, painting, and carpentry.

Every fourth Sunday the boys met at Kawaiaha'o Church Recreational Center on Mission Lane to discuss club affairs. All paid 50 cents dues a month to help the diving boys who were unemployed and needed help.

The dream of this picturesque group of island boys was to have a clubhouse, a dream they never realized. They wanted little, but on the priority list was an enclosed dressing room, especially when the boys were "freezing cold" with blue lips and shivering bodies after their early morning swims. All they ever had were three nails to hang their jackets on, above the shoes or slippers they left on the curbing. And with no place to shower before walking or busing miles to home.

But the boys never complained, a police officer told me. They'd spit out the coins in their mouths and count up the ante, beaming because they had something to take home. And they always sang as they unwound the cast-off flower leis from their heads and shook the salt water from long sideburned locks and wiggled into tattered khaki jackets that barely covered their soaking swim shorts.

They were all off within minutes, some to fishnets, some to pick and shovel, some to kitchen sinks, and others to the nearest newsstand to read the want ads for jobs.

Nostalgia

Gone is the familiar multiethnicity of my childhood, when guttural Hawaiian and Oriental languages were heard more than English on the streetcar; gone is the old Chinese man who took his trolley fare coin out of his ear with his long little fingernail; gone are the Japanese girls with hair below their waists clasped with tin barrettes, and their mothers in beautiful silk kimonos, and the Chinese grandmas in black silk pajamas and real jade in 24-karat gold, the Filipina ladies in *piña* (pineapple) cloth blouses and the men in barongs, the Koreans in high-bodiced gowns of pea green and fuchsia silk, and silver and gold ornaments in their thick, long black hair neatly coiffed above their ears.

Gone are the gleaming white ships on the Pacific that we students crossed for $65 while we sang on deck all night with our 'ukuleles until the San Francisco fog made us hoarse. Gone are the "Boat Days" when the whole town closed shops and sauntered down Fort and Bishop Streets to buy leis, "two-for-a-quatta" plumeria, 50 cents carnation; the Royal Hawaiian Band and falsettos songs when everybody cried, coming or going to the cold gray mainland.

And gone are the nights on the spacious lawn as we were rocked to sleep in our lanai hammock, as the beachboys played steel guitars and 'ukuleles and sang Hawaiian songs for our visitors.

Today, as I run around my tree house in Lanikai barefoot, I look out to the open sea fringed with coco palms and a few houses in sight and recall my childhood in Hawai'i with a nostalgia that is real and lasting.

I tell my grandkids the island legends I heard from that *kupuna* in Kaimuki when I heard the steam shovel making roads, now wiped out by the H-1 Freeway East!

As a *kupuna* today, I find my bare toes still pliable enough to pick up a mangrove root on the sand and write words and draw pictures in the foamy shore break for the grandchildren to read. And recently, when I had a deaf-mute friend visit and could not communicate in signs and was without a pad and pencil at the beach, I wrote again with my toes holding the mangrove root. He smiled and wrote back with the same smooth, brown-and-green seed pod that had floated miles across the sea to root itself in brackish water and form a new swamp.

Ours is a fragile group of islands, the farthest from land all around than any others on our planet.

When I swim at Waikiki, I face seaward and it is the same as before, where fascinating tropical fish swim in and out of coral and the waves break for waiting canoes and surfers. I see the same *manini, kihikihi,* parrotfish, goatfish, squirrelfish, *papio, ulua,* eels, stingrays, nudibranch, sea worms, sea cucumber, octopus, squid, and waving green seaweedy grasses tucked in and out of beds of bright yellow, purple, red, and pure white coral reaching up for sunlight.

Today the high-rises in Honolulu bother me. The horizon is still a line of indigo blue but with fewer big ships.

I feel sun on my skin and warm myself enough to smooth out the bluish crinkly wrinkles of being too long in the sea. I step on smooth, and not-so-smooth rocks that make creases in my feet and penetrate through to make me bleed. But I get to shore before I realize I am cut by sharp coral and am bleeding. I bleed, too, inside my heart now when I look up and see the towering monstrosities of progress surrounding me. So I turn around again and swim out to sea to cleanse the soul within me.

Epilogue

It is all changed—the land I knew
as a child long ago,
or is it I who have changed
in living past the time I knew?
Nostalgia haunts and penetrates
the mind, and illuminates
sharp vignettes I behold
lest they, too, be bulldozed o'er;
No building cranes loomed in the sky,
no stressed concrete, no girded beams
mounted suites like honeycombs
sucked dry of nectar we did taste;
saccharin sweet to our lips
were blossoms growing,
not cement!
As buildings rise, my spirit sinks
and once again I close my eyes
and revel in my memories...

About the Author

Peggy Hickok Hodge is a published writer of Hawaiiana and other feature stories for the past 60 years for both Hawaiian and mainland press and magazines.

She has also authored four books: *Home Gardens in Hawaii* (Tongg 1958), *Favorite Hawaiian Legends* (Tongg 1961), *Tropical Gardening* (Tuttle 1971), and *Gardening in Hawaii* (Mutual Publishing 1997).

Mrs. Hodge, born in Honolulu during World War I, grew up barefoot in Hawai'i and in this book recalls the early days of her childhood and the times in Hawai'i after her parents came here from California in 1910.

She currently writes feature stories, usually with a humorous twist, for local and mainland press and magazines. Many of her published stories are reprinted in various mainland anthologies of Hawaiian history.

The book is illustrated with many historical photos, some of which are printed here for the first time.